For Jacky and Oscar

Contents

1. Meeting the Queen

That Friday was a summer day—July 6th 2001. I was invited to Her Majesty the Queen's reception for a celebration of thirty years of Chinese education in Edinburgh.

In the morning, I opened my camphor wood trunk.

Those scents again, filling the living room, had never changed even a little after years and years. The wooded mountains, the ravine streams, my mother's breast, my little sister's milky-sweet aroma; they came faintly from seemingly far away.

'The Queen must wear red,' I thought.

I finally chose a dark teal green silk quilted *cheongsam* dress instead of my favourite one in gold. Golden clothes used to be only worn by kings in China. It was a royal colour.

People always say the *cheongsam* is the 'poem' of the Chinese woman. That dress would be the most sophisticated, handmade in Hong Kong by a famous *cheongsam* maker. It would just lie on your body beautifully, no matter if you had a slender waist or a fuller figure. A well-cut *cheongsam* expressed a woman's virtuousness, elegance, and gentleness. I called it magic clothes. I knew I would look good and feel good.

I closed the trunk, the copper-mounted corners still fitting perfectly in place. The scent faded slowly, like the wind, like the breeze.

Two months prior, I had been selected by members of the Chinese Community Association in Edinburgh to be the first person in the queue in the reception line.

'Aunty Doris, you are the most suitable person to be the first to meet the Queen,' said the chair, Mr Lau who was well known by the Chinese community and the city council.

On that sunny day with some showers—typical Scottish weather in the summer—my taxi was on the way to the city hall on the hill of the Royal Mile where I would meet the Queen.

I was thinking of a little story in the fifties in Hong Kong.

My husband Andrew, in his sergeant uniform, was hanging his hat and said with a smile, 'Darling, today Jimmy said his wife Susie was found by the police because she was invited to Her Majesty's yacht, *Britannia*, as a special guest to have a meal.'

'Oh really?' I was surprised. Susie was one of those girls who used to work on Prince Philip's ship, HMS *Tamar*. They cleaned, washed and painted. She was given a lot of sweets.

'We joked with Jimmy that his wife was Philip's dream lover,' Andrew said.

We couldn't hold in our laughter. Jimmy was Andrew's colleague. He was a naval officer during the war. He joined the Hong Kong police instead of coming back to England. He married a Tanka girl, Susie, whose family lived on the boats for generations.

Jimmy was famously very good at swimming. He could easily cross the water between the Hong Kong islands and Stonecutters Island, Ngong Shuen Chau, where there was an important naval base and where my husband worked once.

I still remember that day, down to what was on our dinner table—it was wok-grilled whole bream, char siu, the roasted pork, and fried water spinach with spicy bean curd, called Chinese cheese. Our nine-year-old adorable daughter was wearing a sky-blue dress with yellow and white chrysanthemums, her new favourite dress that I had made for her.

It was May 1959, a lovely evening. I couldn't help but wonder if our Queen knew about Susie.

The taxi finally stopped outside the city hall.

'Seven pounds please.' The driver looked younger than my daughter.

'I don't think so, it is always five pounds,' I insisted.

'Your kind of immigrants should pay more,' he replied as he looked at me from the mirror.

'Your free school meals were on my tax bills I paid,' I said.

The taxi driver couldn't say anything. He took five pounds.

The Queen walked in slowly with her iconic warm smile. She wore a long pink blossom floral dress, almost as I had guessed. It surprised me that the Queen was much prettier than she was on the television. Her face looked extremely soft, it seemed to have no wrinkles at all, like an egg that had just been peeled out of its shell.

Seven years younger than me, the Queen walked toward me. I curtsied.

'How long have you been in England?' she asked after I rose from my curtsy.

'Since 1946.'

'Oh, quite a while,' the Queen smiled, 'I hope you are happy in my country.'

'Yes, Your Majesty.'

2. An Unwanted Girl

2.1. A Baby Girl Was Born

My name is May Oi. Beautiful words with beautiful meanings: 'pretty' and 'love'. I was named by my grandfather.

The day I was born, he said to my father, 'A girl?' He hummed on his opium bed, 'Girls should be born last, not first. Call her... *May Oi.*' In Cantonese, the pronunciation matched my grandfather's meaning completely: 'The girl should come last, not first'.

That was 1919, in Hong Kong.

Not long after Hong Kong was named Hong Kong from an unknown village, my grandfather's father arrived to do business with people from the Hou family village, Heng Tin. My great-grandfather was a very smart man. The Hou businesses, in addition to the silk shops on Up and Down Nine Road in Guangzhou, included a mine in Guangxi. However, the main business was in Hong Kong and consisted of three flour and rice shops for both wholesale and retail. They were all named using the most important words for business, like 'booming', 'lucky' and 'success'.

In the early nineteenth century, the wheat flour industry was the second largest industry in China. Due to the decrease in the import of foreign wheat flour and the increase in European demand, Chinese flour was exported in large quantities to Britain, France, the United States, Japan and Southeast Asia. The flour industry was a very profitable business at the time.

Grandfather became a rich man in his village after many years. He had the nickname 'Eight Million Hou', because he was the eighth of his father's children.

The Hou family's largest flour and rice shop was located on Sheung Wan Road on Hong Kong Island, a very busy north-south regional business trading street. The three-storey wood and brick building was also my home. The trading shop was on the ground floor and outside the arcade. My grandfather's office was in the shop's side room.

When an important buyer came, my grandfather would come out of his room, ask his servant to make a nice pot of tea, sit by the well-made rosewood round table in the middle of the shop and talk. The kitchen and dining living room behind the patio yard were right in the middle of the building. Light and rain came from the sky.

My father's seven or eight caged canaries were hung from a bamboo pole on the patio; they sang happily, non-stop every day. There were warehouses on both sides of the patio. Bags of flour and rice were hoarded into piles like hills. A few strong men would come in and out carrying big bags of wheat flour, pouring with sweat in the summer.

My favourite game was playing hide-and-seek in the flour shop with my aunts and my younger brother Gok. Once, I found a very hidden place. The flour hill next to the wall left a big gap, just enough for me to move in. No one knew about it, and no one could find me even when they looked round and round. They ran to Grandfather's room and asked if he saw me. He took off his gold framed glasses and said, 'May Oi? She broke my gold pen yesterday. She hasn't paid me back yet. I haven't seen that kind of naughty girl before—she is not even like a girl. Why didn't she grow a little bit more in her mother's stomach to be a boy? Get out and ask her to come to see me.'

'May Oi, May Oi, you are dead this time, Grandfather wants you to get out to see him,' my Number Ten Aunt shouted deliberately. I didn't dare show up. I was scared thinking of my grandfather's cane, a chicken feather sweeper, which most likely was used more to beat children instead of clean dust and spiderwebs.

I don't know for how long I stayed in that secret corner. I was called by my mother's gentle voice in a dream: 'May Oi, good girl, come out quickly.' I opened my eyes to see my mother's curved eyebrows. She was kneeling on the ground, reaching out her hand to me. 'Oh, look at you, you are covered in white flour.' Mother bent down and patted my water-brush-red satin dress gown, wiping my face with her handkerchief embroidered with lotus flowers.

She said softly, 'May Oi, remember, your hair can't be messed up like this, it's not ladylike. We are waiting for you to eat. Come.' Mother walked in front of me, her dark green gown, long, down to her knees, covering half her white trousers. She wore fashionably styled pointed-toed black leather shoes and her petite body swayed—she looked like a princess in the Cantonese opera.

Every month, my mother would ask Fa, one of our housekeepers, to shave her face. Fa used two very thin ropes to roll back and forth on Mother's face. My mother soon had two clean eyebrows and a neat hairline, like a fairy in a painting. I asked my mother to shave my face and eyebrows. She said, 'Silly girl, not until the day you get married.'

2.2. My Mother

My mother married into the Hou family at the age of fifteen, but actually, she was only fourteen by the traditional Chinese calendar count, which always added one year to your birth age. She became the wife of the fourth young master in the eighth house of the Hou family. She was the daughter-in-law of the most well-known, virtuous and able woman in the village.

My mother was the eldest daughter of a comfortable family whose surname, Sung, was from a neighbouring village. She had a marriage agreement ever since she was the age of five with my father who was age seven.

Their marriage was well arranged by their parents. They had never formally met before the marriage and could not even mention each other in front of people if they didn't want to be gossiped about. Intimacy between men and women in any public place was a disgrace. This was what was taught by girls' parents and their parents' parents, going back thousands of years.

On the wedding day, the Hou family sent a beautiful sedan carriage decorated with silk flowers to the Sung home, carried by eight men. The carriage would be sat in only once in a woman's life. She would be very proud to tell everyone that she was transported to her husband's home by an eight-man-carried sedan carriage. It meant she was the first wife of her husband and had power and supreme status above her husband's other wives. Her children too.

From the moment my mother stepped out of this carriage and across the threshold of the Hou family's big main door, she became Hou property, and they gave her the right to release her feet that had been wrapped and tied by fabric.

A lot of girls sobbed as they were forced into a foot binding both day and night; they had to wrap their feet as early as three years old because this beauty ideal was booming at the time of the end of the Ming and the beginning of the Qing Dynasty. No matter poor or wealthy, women with small feet were highly desirable. Men were amused by women's tiny little shoes. They also believed the way women walked with tiny feet created a better body, which they found more enjoyable.

After the marriage agreement was made between the Hous and the Sungs, my grandfather sent a message to the Sung family: his future daughter-in-law did not have to bind her feet to as small as three inches, like a golden lotus flower, but they were not to be as big as dragon boats. The Sung family wrapped their daughter's feet very carefully to match the Hou family's request.

My mother's feet had to be wrapped, but only at night up until the day before her marriage. Luckily she was not in much pain. Her feet were small, but she could wear heeled leather shoes. They were always polished and shiny.

I mostly remember my mother's smells. The camellia tree from her hair. The smell of camphor wood from her pyjamas, faintly unforgettable like a forest after sun and rain—so strong, so refreshing.

My mother's hair was deep black, shiny and carefully taken care of. She always said that girls are not humanlike with messy hair. Hair became something in my life I could not take lightly.

Every time my mother wanted to wash her hair, Fa would smash off a piece of sediment from the camellia tree. This sediment was made to into a big, flat solid cake, then boiled in hot water. A towel was used to separate the residue. The water would be a clean, light brown. This kind of shampoo was used widely in Southern China; it could stop itching and dandruff and give your hair a shiny, silky look.

'Mrs Hou, it's ready now,' Fa shouted with her strong Nanhai accent when the water temperature was just right. The copper water basin was placed on a wooden shelf by the patio.

My mother elegantly bent over. Her long hair was soaked in the large basin. She closed her eyes and rubbed her hair gently with her hands. When it was over, she stretched out her hand and called me: 'May Oi, hand me a towel.' She looked down and dried her hair. I squatted down to see her flushed face. Water dropped on my face, warm and fragrant.

Before my mother went to bed, she took down her hair bun, sat in front of the vanity mirror, and combed her hair. The foreign-style ivory, oval-shaped comb bought for her by my father was very pretty and delicate, with foreign beauties painted on the handle and matching mirrors on the back. She always put it back in the box carefully after she was done.

I lay in her arms in bed, her hair as soft as her silk pyjamas, the fragrance from her wrapping me up around.

All my mother's silk and wool clothes had to be folded carefully and tidied up inside a large camphor wood trunk. She insisted on folding them herself, not Fa.

In traditional Chinese culture, we believe the camphor tree has tenacious vitality. It represents auspiciousness, longevity, happiness and harmony. Since ancient times, its bark, fruits and wood have been used as medicines. These easily-grown trees can survive for thousands of years.

The father would plant a camphor tree when his daughter was born. The tree would grow up with the daughter in excellent shades of green until she married. The strong stump of the camphor tree would become the wood of a large trunk. This would be the best gift, a must-have from parents to daughter on her wedding day. The fragrance of the camphor wood would remain forever. It would stop all moths and damp. Their daughter's most important belongings would be safe for a long, long time.

My mother's camphor trunk was carved all over with phoenixes, cranes and peony flowers, the four corners covered with glistening copper. It was beautiful.

After my brothers were born, my mother would accompany me to sleep only when I had a fever; only then could I sleep with her and my father.

I shared a room with Choi, another housekeeper. She was about fifteen years old. Her snoring was like thunder, and she often talked loudly in her sleep. Once she yelled: 'May Oi, get up and pee!'

One night, I quietly got up, opened her mosquito net, and put a big piece of salt in her mouth. The big salt was hidden in my bed for a few days, but I couldn't wake up to tease her. That night, I decided to drink a pot of my grandfather's premium oolong tea to keep my eyes open until Choi started talking in her dreams.

Those days in Hong Kong were happy memories.

2.3. Leaving Hong Kong for the Village Home

One day, my mother was packing. She said, 'Girl, we are leaving Hong Kong for our village home. It is your grandfather's intention.' I saw her melancholy in her eyes. I had been living in Hong Kong ever since I started to have memories.

I only went back to my village home for Chinese New Year and for the very traditional feasts of worship for ancestors, or relatives' weddings or elders' big birthdays. But it was always a good time.

'Your grandfather said, your father... It isn't good for him, to stay in Hong Kong. Going back to the village home will be good for us. Don't forget that it is our root home,' my mother said.

Three days later, my family took an overnight boat trip and returned to Heng Tin Village. I was seven years old that year.

A few years later my grandfather also returned to Heng Tin Village because he lost a lot of money. I was told by my aunties that there was a *gweilo*, a Western foreigner, involved.

I remember there was a foreigner who would come to our Hong Kong home. He spoke Cantonese and he also spoke English with my grandfather. Grandfather would ask Choi to serve tea and some biscuits while they were sitting around the table in the front living room. A few of us children would play around the table.

While Grandfather and the foreigner were looking down at the account books, I would reach out, take a salted biscuit and stuff it quickly into my mouth. Sometimes, the foreigner would smile and take out a few big silver coins from his pocket to give to us before he left.

Later, when the foreigner came again he went into my grandfather's room. We only took a peek through the door and waited for him to come out. Then later, the door closed behind them. After that, I never saw the foreigner again.

Years later, I learned that the foreigner's surname was Ho, the most well-known, and the first Chinese allowed to live at the Victoria Peak in Hong Kong. He was one of the brothers in the Ho family's third generation. He worked as a buyer for the largest British-owned company in Hong Kong, Jardine Matheson. Because he was too smart, the company became concerned about him. They intentionally left a detailed false statement on the table which stated that the company's share price would rise sharply. He thought he knew the latest secret stock market information that no one else knew and excitedly informed his brother. As well as emptying their own wallets, they also persuaded all of their friends and their friends' friends to invest and place bets.

A few days later, Jardine Matheson's share price plummeted. A setup, this trap resulted in the loss of all their money along with their investors' money, including my grandfather's last properties in Hong Kong, the three flour shops and our home. That was the first stock market disaster in Hong Kong.

The Ho brothers went bankrupt overnight and owed a large number of debts to a lot of people. Two of them committed suicide, one by poison, and one by gun. The oldest cashed all his assets to try and pay his debts, but it wasn't enough. One night, he fled from Hong Kong to Vietnam with some of his family members. This descendant of the Ho family was very clever and courageous and became a gambling tycoon. He famously took four wives and had eighteen children all together—one less wife than my grandfather.

3. My Village Home

3.1. The Fish Pond

My hometown village, Heng Tin, in the Namhoi county of Guangdong, was in South China, near Hong Kong. Namhoi was an important region at that time. Once the first trading port with the Western world in the Qing Empire, the Thirteen Factories in Guangzhou were under the Namhoi Regional Government's administration. It was also a region where there was cultivation of rice and fish by the Pearl River Delta, meaning it was a rich, living resource.

Everyone born in the village are Hou descendants. The surname is Hou. We all have the same forefathers going back hundreds of years. The names of all males are written down in a book which is enshrined in the Hou ancestral hall at the entrance of the village. Only those who have committed a great humiliation to the family are disallowed entry into the family ancestral hall to worship their ancestors, their names struck from the genealogical record. Girls' names however, aren't on the record.

At the ancestral hall, which we called the 'head' of the village, there was a huge banyan tree planted by our ancestors. Walk from the ancestral hall along a long narrow road, which becomes wider and wider when entering the main part of the village, and you will see a large patio for drying grain in the sun, used by children to play around.

On its left, there was a big fishpond. A *gweilo* friend of my father came to visit one day and suggested to my grandfather to fill the fishpond up. He said this uncovered lake is very dangerous for the children having fun nearby.

'This is not a lake. You don't even see fatty fish in the water.' Grandfather was sitting on the slippery smooth rosewood chair in the living room, counting his large Buddhist beads in his hand, speaking sullenly in English. But, he did then later ask someone to build a low brick wall.

Our house was the largest in our village, right at the front, facing the large patio. It was always kept closed by large dark red heavy wooden doors. Both sides had a big bronze lion head, rings hung from their noses as door handles. The right-hand side lion was shinier than the left one because it was used much more. Behind the door, there were two thick long square-shaped wooden bolts on the upper and lower part of the door, both of them capped in copper on the ends.

At night, when I was lying on the bed, I often heard a heavy thudding noise. It was one of our servants pulling down the door latch and pushing the sliding gate fence stored on the left to the right. The heavy gate was made of twelve hardwood poles, as thick as adult arms. It would be firmly perfectly embedded into the twelve holes in the wall, making a dull sound. It was used to guard against robbery. On some humid summer days, we kept the door open, leaving the gate shut.

When he was done he usually coughed lightly for some reason. I would hear the sound of his wooden clogs walking through the corridor outside my bedroom further and further away, then I would fall asleep.

The house was built with solid dark green bricks, which were of the best quality. Grandfather built one for each of his four sons before he died. The houses were built all around Grandfather's house.

As the fourth son, my father was given a three-bedroom detached house behind my grandfather's third son, whose house was behind my grandfather's. His other two sons' houses were on the left and right, in better locations—and bigger.

Between these houses, there were beautiful wooden arches with ornaments and words of blessing engraved into the wood. They are still there today. Each house had a pair of ornate solid wood doors. Big copper handles hung heavily from the lions' noses on both sides, just smaller than my grandfather's.

I liked the sound when the door was opened—deep, solid; it meant my father had come home from being out.

Mother would smile and say to us, 'Go to bed now, May Oi, and Gok—watch your brother Kai.' She held the kerosene lamp, sending us to our room which was on the other side of the living room. We would see our shadows on the wall of the living room. Kai, my youngest brother, was always afraid of those shadows.

3.2. My Grandfather's Five Wives

My grandfather had five wives in total. Ten children survived. Four sons, and six daughters. His youngest daughter, my Number Ten Aunt, was only about one year older than me. The household was taken care of by my grandfather's fifth wife, as I remember. I called her Sam Ma—it meant 'Number Three Grandmother'.

Two of my grandfather's wives didn't have the title of 'Grandmother', because they were only women who had children with my grandfather, but were not formally married. Only one of them was my father's mother—my true grandmother.

Grandfather's first wife died after she gave birth to a son. At the same time, Grandfather had a concubine. She had a private housemaid, who came the same day Grandfather married her. Everyone knew her role. She was a housemaid who had special duties, which were to serve the husband by having intercourse with him on behalf of the hostess during her periods of menstruation or pregnancy, so that she would not need to worry about her husband soliciting prostitution or frequenting social clubs of this kind.

When these housemaids were no longer needed, they would usually end up marrying whoever their hostess thought was good for them. However, she was a lucky one because her hostess died after she gave birth to two sons. She then became my grandfather's Number Three Wife, but she couldn't be called 'Grandmother'. She was, however, the most fertile of Grandfather's wives. She gave birth to two boys and four girls. One of her sons was my father.

I heard that she suffered from gout and died in pain. Before she died, all her joints were swollen, her skin was stretched to the point of thinness, her purple veins were visible, and she dared not move. She was my grandfather's favourite because he specifically hired a professional mourner for her funeral. 'Her cry was cadenced and rich in sorrow with words of praise and memories. She seemed like one of our family members,' I heard once.

Grandfather then married his Number Four Wife who had no children and had a short life. She passed away less than a year later.

The last wife my grandfather was married to took her title and became a decent third grandmother to the Hou family's next generation. I called her Number Three Grandmother—Sam Ma. Though she was just one of the servants, she would be buried with my grandfather after her death. Her surname would be written into the Hou ancestral book, followed by my grandfather's other two wives. She was the only one of my grandfather's wives who had big feet, as they were not bound. Despite some of the Hou children's mothers being only humble women, their children weren't treated any differently. They learned how to be well-behaved and how to read and write.

3.3. Xin Sang's Complaint

Grandfather hired a teacher to home tutor his children and grandchildren. A decent middle-aged man, wearing plastic glasses that had broken arms, came three times a week. We called him Xin Sang respectfully, meaning 'teacher'. He was teaching us from the *Three Character Primer*, mainly just through recitation and writing and rewriting the old book's words again and again:

'Man on earth, good at birth. The same nature varies on nurture.'

'With no education, there'd be aberration.'

'To teach well, you deeply dwell.'

This was thousand-year-old, very traditional Chinese philosophy. My grandfather insisted we must remember it for the rest of our lives. He was so right—I have never forgotten.

One day, Xin Sang complained to my grandfather, 'May Oi is bright and has a good memory. She passes all the tests. But she just can't sit still. Today she threw a tangerine core at me and blamed Gok.'

My brother Gok studied hard, but forgot words while revising those boring books—often he shed tears in anxiety. I hated that Gok couldn't remember those words even though he knew them, and I also hated that Xin Sang beat his hands. I threw those cores at Xin Sang when he raised his voice at Gok.

My grandfather closed his eyes and listened intently to Xin Sang's complaint. Then he shook his head and sighed. Turning his head, he said to me, 'If you misbehave again, you will be spanked with a cane, and you will not be allowed to go to class.'

I was quite happy with what Grandfather said, wishing that I could now play mahjong with my aunts, and learn how to knit jumpers and scarves. No more need to repeat those boring words thousands of times.

But when Grandfather decided to send my two younger brothers to a private school in town, unexpectedly he asked me to go with them. 'Go, learn how to write a family letter, that will be enough for you. Your aunts are all just preparing to marry,' he said, sitting under the crystal candle chandelier. He looked at me, 'May Oi, you are not stupid.'

On the first day of school, my mother told Choi to tie a spring onion by my heart, because the word's pronunciation meant 'intelligent'; to put a *lin gok* (a water caltrop), the Cantonese pronunciation of which meant 'smart', into the left pocket of my trousers; to put a boiled egg in my right trouser pocket for good memory; and to hang a small mirror on my back for seeing and thinking clearly.

'May Oi, remember to listen to Xin Sang. When you can read and write, you aren't going to be afraid to travel all over the world,' my mother said, squatting in front of me with a serious face. Her hairline had just been neatly shaven, like a bridge, gently curved.

She took out her handkerchief, put it in the hidden pocket of my jacket, and swept my hair back with her hands. 'Eat eggs and *lin gok* when you are hungry.' She was smiling.

My mother could not read or write, but she had a good memory and could recognise a lot of characters. She could also count very well.

That day, it was Choi who carried me on her back walking to school. This meant that in the future, I would become someone who didn't need to walk, but would sit in a carriage.

I ended up walking halfway—I wouldn't say I liked the sweat on Choi's back.

3.4. Crying on Her Wedding

My six aunts' biggest hobbies were playing mahjong and learning how to be good wives. They always had reasons not to go to Xin Sang's class. Grandfather said: 'You are all helpless, just like the lazy fisherman—three days of fishing and two days of sunning the nets.' Of course, because they were daughters of the Hou family, when they got married, they were all to be treated decently by my grandfather.

Grandfather would insist that his daughters' husbands send a beautiful gold and red flower carriage. On the wedding day, a strong horse would lead at the front. Following behind would be the wedding team, who would carry my aunt's trousseau. A large camphor wood trunk was always carried behind the carriage. They were made by a good trunk maker following my grandfather's orders. All the Hou girls' important belongings were tied up very well inside by their mothers and grandmothers. My aunts had to be protected by the setting up of a dowry for their future. At the least, they wouldn't be looked down on by their husband's family.

The wedding procession would be from the head of the village to the end of the village. Calves, chickens, geese, ducks, and big fat pigs would all be tied with red ribbons and someone would light firecrackers non-stop. Everyone in the village would be joyous.

However, crying would come from my aunt, first from her room, and then from her carriage. The bride must show how heartbroken she is that she has to marry, that she is reluctant to give up her relatives, and is even more sad that she cannot be filial to her parents at home.

When my fourth aunt, Sei Gu, got married I was nine years old and insisted I join the bridesmaids' team which included my other three aunts and two cousins. We walked for more than an hour and kept our faces looking sad.

I was really sad in fact, because apart from my mother, Sei Gu was the person who loved me the most. She was the eldest daughter of our Hou family.

That night we all stayed in Sei Gu's new home. Six girls squeezed into two big wooden beds. They whispered and laughed all night. They told me to go to sleep and said children were not supposed to be listening.

The next morning, I saw Sei Gu sitting on the edge of the bed with a smile. She was just sixteen years old. I didn't understand why Sei Gu was willing to marry a man who was so bucktoothed. I couldn't help but keep wondering if pretty Sei Gu knew her future husband would turn out like that, whether she would still want to marry him.

Sei Gu held my hand and said to me, 'May Oi, when you get married, I will dress you in a water-red dress, just like mine, and embroider a golden phoenix on it'.

'Don't you know that May Oi can't find anyone to match with yet?' my fifth aunt said.

'Sooner or later, May Oi will meet someone,' my kind-hearted eighth aunt said with a wink.

'The blind woman said that May Oi would marry far away from home and travel across the ocean,' my fifth aunt said. 'Her mother brought details of May Oi's birth time and date to this woman just before the New Year.'

Then my quiet seventh aunt said, 'May Oi always crosses the sea when she travels between Heng Tin and Hong Kong. May Oi likes Hong Kong.'

Only then did I know that I was the only girl in our family who was not matched up with her future husband.

Just as we were talking, my new uncle walked into the room and said shyly, 'Breakfast is ready, let's go out and eat in the dining room.' There was a table full of delicious delicacies.

Suddenly, in came a short and quick woman. Cheerful and loud, she said, 'We are blessed by our ancestors—see, the red.' She looked at us and said giggling, 'As I said, our family is going to have a decent girl as a daughter-in-law. We aren't surprised, she is from the Hou house.'

Except for me, all the girls lowered their heads, blushed and smiled. When I was older, I learned what 'see red' meant. The next morning would be a day of humiliation for the family if a groom couldn't show his family a piece of white cloth with a few drops of blood on it to prove his bride was a pure virgin. If not, the ensuing life for this bride would be full of shame. She would never be elevated to be head of her family committee because of this stigma.

The happy, short and quick woman picked some of the best bits of the meal and placed them in a big bowl, filling it as full as possible. 'For the bride. She deserves it,' she said.

It turned out that the shy bride would stay in the room for three days before she could come out to daily life.

3.5. Beautiful Cousin Yuk Lan

Yuk Lan means 'white jade magnolia', a beautiful girl's name. She was the cousin I envied the most because she went to a girls secondary school. She liked to wear a white top and a black skirt and was proud to be recognised as a pupil of the school. Yuk Lan was my eldest uncle's only daughter with his late wife. She was sent to Guangzhou as my youngest uncle's adopted daughter when she was about ten years old. It was my eldest uncle's new wife's idea.

She spoke in a soft voice and had a sensitive and obedient personality. She was always the quiet one.

Yuk Lan met a boy in Guangzhou who was from our neighbouring village—a perfect match. The first granddaughter of the Hou family married, of course, respectably.

One day, soon after their wedding, Yuk Lan and her new husband returned to their village home by boat from Guangzhou. When Yuk Lan crossed the boat's bridge, her feet slipped; her husband hurriedly reached out to hold her up, and she fell into her husband's arms and chest.

This intimate contact between husband and wife became the most gossiped-about story among fellow villagers, each one telling the other that she was shameful and conspicuous. The story grew more and more outrageous than the original. She felt unwelcome everywhere. Finally, she dared not even leave the house.

I remember that morning, I was playing hopscotch on the large patio outside my house. I saw Yuk Lan holding a bamboo rattan bag, she wore a straw hat like those Hong Kong dwellers.

'May Oi,' she called, 'look at you, sweating too much.'

I jumped on one leg and said, 'Cousin Yuk Lan, you have a pretty hat. Grandfather is in his smoke room, and the aunties are playing mahjong in the hall. Go find them.'

I thought Yuk Lan would be staying for lunch. But I saw her soon after, walking out of the house. Sei Gu followed her behind, but I couldn't hear what they were talking about as they were whispering.

Yuk Lan wiped her eyes with her handkerchief, bowed her head and left. It turned out that Grandfather didn't want to see her.

I went home and saw a box of soda crackers on the big round table in the living room. It was Grandfather's favourite snack. I knew that Yuk Lan must have bought it at Sincere Department Store where my grandfather loved to shop when he was in Hong Kong. The owner chose the name 'Sincere' for the purpose of honesty; there you could find almost every product from Europe and America. I always thought my mother could have been one of their saleswomen—it'd be better if she sold shoes. I could see that my most adorable cousin was so keen to please our grandfather.

I opened it secretly and ate two pieces. My aunts' joyful laughter came from the mahjong room.

Sam Ma was teaching Choi to stuff dace fish in the kitchen, 'You just never get it, do you? Remember to be careful when you start with the fish skin. Crush the fish meat and put some egg whites in it, then vigorously stir it until it is gelatinised. Otherwise, it won't be as tender and crispy.' She always kept her voice loud and determined, telling people who was in charge of this house.

Grandfather's room door was closed.

That night, Yuk Lan hung herself in her bedroom.

She used the red ribbon, which was made into a large peony and worn on the groom's chest on the day of the wedding.

'I told her don't take the gossip too hard; stand straight, and never mind those shadows slanting,' Sei Gu said to us, tearfully. 'Father should have seen her—even if he just shouted at her, or beat her… And I should have walked home with her.'

Since then, I never saw my oldest uncle return to the village. Nor his youngest brother, who raised Yuk Lan as his own.

3.6. The Kidnapper's Gold Tooth

In my grandfather's mind, his youngest son was the most capable and charming one. He was responsible for the Hou family's mine in Guangxi and the silk shop in Up and Down Nine Road of Guangzhou. He rarely came home.

I called him Luk Suk, which meant he was my grandfather's sixth child. Luk Suk liked to travel extensively and liked to make friends. He would often wear shiny silk satin clothes, place more than three golden pens in his pockets, and swagger down the street with a big cigarette in his mouth. All amusement places knew the sixth master of the Hou family.

As a result, he was often kidnapped. When the kidnappers walked into the village they strutted around like they owned the place. 'Does anyone know Eight Million Hou?' they shouted. The whole village knew then that Luk Suk was in trouble again.

Two or three kidnappers with big swords in their hands stood outside our main doors but were obstructed by the wooden cage. They reported their names and where they came from, spread out a letter from Luk Suk, and discussed with our servant Dong the conditions and the ransom they were asking for. Then they were invited to see my grandfather in his private room. This side room was where Grandfather smoked opium and it was also the place where his grandchildren stayed with him the most.

He smoked while bargaining with the kidnappers and did not seem angry at all. After the negotiations were completed, he gave a signal. Sam Ma went to the bedroom on the right side of the living room to open the bed and from a deep hidden narrow compartment took money out from a wooden box. This specially made compartment was just wide enough for my grandfather to roll into when needed.

Outside, the kids pretended to feed the goldfish around the big fish pot on the patio, but moreover were watching the excitement.

Money in hand, the kidnappers grinned. The culprit bowed and thanked my grandfather, 'Wishing you longevity.' My grandfather let out a deep sigh.

One kidnapper even gave us some lucky coins. He opened his mouth wide and said, '*Lei si*, come, here; children, grow up quickly.' I looked at his big golden tooth and badly wanted to pull it out with iron tongs.

As my grandfather got older and older, Luk Suk had almost lost the family fortune. The last time Luk Suk was kidnapped, my grandfather really couldn't pay in full.

The head of the kidnappers saw our new housekeeper, Jin, standing on a chair cleaning the chandelier. He said, 'I want her to be my wife, as part of your son's ransom.' Jin almost fell, she was terrified and cried.

Sam Ma's finger pointed at him and shouted, 'A man should have rules and behave well. You only came for money. My maid is a good girl. If you want to marry her, send your matchmaker.' I have never known where my Sam Ma's strength came from.

Sure enough, a few days later, the kidnapper sent a matchmaker to propose marriage. Jin, who was nineteen years old, was married to the kidnapper from my home to cover half of Luk Suk's ransom. Luckily, Jin was well adored by her husband. I finally felt relief from worrying about her. Sam Ma quietly told me that there was a red mole on Jin's belly. It meant she was a girl with luck.

Luk Suk died five years after his father passed away, at age one hundred and three. He died in one of the fourteen-month-long Japanese bombings in Guangzhou, along with his wife. Our shops were also destroyed, and mine closed.

The Hou family was declining seriously.

4. Broken Home

4.1. Soaking in Blood

It was late autumn, the golden rice fields around our village were full of yellow rice ears half bending down, and the villagers were preparing for harvest.

Sam Ma was busy dealing with the farmers. Our few remaining rice fields badly needed to be reaped and threshed on time.

My mother was giving birth to her fourth child. She spent a day and a night in the room quietly until I heard the baby cry. It was so loud. Sam Ma and the woman we called the midwife hurriedly entered and exited the room, while my father sat in the living room, weeping.

Three days later, I went into the room to see my mother. Her face was as white as white paper, and her lips were smoky grey. Her black hair was draped neatly over her back, stuck together greasily.

'May Oi, you have a younger sister now. In the future, treat each other as companions and discuss girl things.' Mother ruffled my fringe affectionately. 'Look at your hair, my girl. Too long and messy. You need a haircut when I get better,' she smiled.

Choi came into the room with a large bamboo steamer, the inside covered with firewood and charcoal. She whispered to my mother, 'Change to this one.'

She uncovered my mother's quilt, and I saw she was sitting on a bamboo steamer, the charcoal inside red and black. Choi pulled it out carefully and replaced it with the new one.

'The chicken soup will be ready soon. I will bring it later,' Choi said. 'Sam Ma said give it a few more days, you won't bleed so much.'

The chickens raised in the courtyard were killed one after another.

The bamboo steamer was changed again and again.

A few more days and a few more days passed.

My mother never got out of her bedroom again.

She never even got up from her bed.

In the middle of that night, I was awakened by a tragic howl. It was my father. The wife of the fourth son of the Hou family, my mother, died of bleeding from childbirth.

She was twenty-eight years old.

The weeping Choi hugged me tightly and said, 'Your mother is truly the wrong person to die. It's like cutting the wrong bamboo.' My arm held onto Gok's shoulder firmly, Kai leaned on him, and we all cried loudly.

My mother was buried by a lake outside the village. Her headstone was shovelled away during a road development project in the past years. No one knows the exact location of her tomb anymore. Gok had written many times to the village, telling them that if bones were found there with a silver coin between the teeth, they could be his mother's. He saw his father putting a silver coin in his wife's mouth before the coffin closed.

But no one could answer him.

The villagers said that the fate of the descendants of those buried by the lake will be mostly to leave home far away, even across the seas and oceans.

4.2. A Red Envelope

Sam Ma believed the baby girl, my little sister, would bring death: she must leave our home forever. I begged her: 'Sam Ma I will raise her.'

'You are not an adult yourself, and you have two younger brothers as well. Look at your father, only feeling sorry for himself. I am worried about how he can put food on his children's table,' Sam Ma sighed deeply. 'Your sister must go. She may die if she stays,' she insisted.

One morning, a middle-aged woman in black came to our home. She wore a bamboo hat that looked like a big pot. She was a Tanka who lived on the boats.

'Choi, bring the baby girl out,' Sam Ma said. 'This baby is very good; doesn't cry much. She can even smile at people at less than two months old—look at her, so cute.'

The woman took my sister carefully and looked at her intently. She inspected her hands and feet. There was a smile on her face.

'Let me change the nappy for her,' she insisted. Sam Ma understood what she meant.

'Oh yes. Choi can show you how to do it,' Sam Ma replied quickly.

Sam Ma asked, 'I was told she will be your first child. No worries. This girl won't cause much trouble, really.' Sam Ma herself had no birth children experience; she didn't know much. She was just worried the woman would change her mind.

Sam Ma raised her hand to call me. 'May Oi, come here.' I was sat in the lower hall. 'May Oi is the baby's sister. She takes good care of her family with skill and great diligence.' Sam Ma held my shoulders and turned me around. I was smiling stupidly and tears were swallowed.

Finally, the woman took out a big red baby back sling with a big peony embroidered on it. She gave a big red envelope to Sam Ma. Inside must have been some money that they had agreed to. Choi packed folded nappies, which were made with flour bags, into a large cloth bag and two big tins of milk powder. 'These nappies are durable,' said Choi. 'Milk, once a day, and feed her rice soup.'

I put a hat on my sister, a hat in pink wool, knit with two rabbit ears on the front which I spent the whole night knitting. Her smell was so sweet, like my mother's. I wished she would open her eyes.

My brother Gok and I stood under the banyan tree, watching our little sister disappear at the end of the road. My father was still in his room, lying on the bed, covered with a quilt.

Our sister still had no name. Everyone just called her 'Baby Girl'.

'When I'm older, I'll find her and get her back, Sister,' nine-year-old Gok said, while wiping away his tears.

Ten years later, Gok met a girl in a quay when he was a boatman on the river.

'She looked so like you, Sister,' he held me, 'and she was about the same age as our little sister. The girl was generous, and felt familiar.'

'My name is Ho So Ping. Our boat is over there,' she told Gok when he quickly stepped forward to ask her name. Gok followed her home to see her parents. He asked the couple bluntly, 'Your daughter was adopted from Heng Tin?' Then he said firmly, 'I want her back, no matter how much you want. I have been looking for her for years.'

'Who said that?' The woman, who was about forty years old, said in a choked voice. 'No, I gave birth to her, I am her mother.'

She turned her face to her daughter who was cooking at the stern of the boat. 'She looks more like her father. If you don't believe me, come tomorrow for dinner.'

'I will steam yellow croaker for you tomorrow,' the girl was very happy while seeing Gok off ashore.

The next morning, Gok carried all his money and couldn't wait to return to the quay.

The boat had disappeared.

The neighbouring boatman told Gok that they left last night in a hurry.

'There was a blue cloth patch on the roof of their boat. I will recognise it,' Gok wrote in a letter to me, 'I am going to keep looking, I may have a chance to see them again.'

In fact, since then, we never saw her again. Steamed yellow croaker fish became Gok's favourite dish.

4.3. Erhu Elegy

In Cantonese feature films, there is always someone in the big family who is an idler. My father was one of them. He never intervened in family affairs. In Hong Kong, he worked in the shop for two or three hours at most. The rest of the day was spent drinking outside, making friends, feeding his canaries, playing mahjong—or gambling, which was his most despised bad habit by our family. That habit was the reason we were sent back to the village from Hong Kong.

He liked to wear Western clothes, wear a tie, and read Western books. Since Grandfather passed away, our home started to separate, divided by the brothers' families. This meant we cooked our own food and we bought our own food too. Only one maid, Choi, stayed to look after Sam Ma.

The money Sam Ma gave, from all that was left from Grandfather, became less and less. Life became more and more difficult.

My father played the erhu very nicely. The erhu is a traditional Chinese instrument and since it first appeared in China during the Tang Dynasty through Mongolia, the most popular one. It is a two-stringed bowed instrument with amazing tonal and dynamic range. It's sometimes known in the Western world as the Chinese violin—but much easier to learn. My father taught himself. He often sat on the big rocks under the big banyan tree and played it in the evening. I don't know how he could remember those notes. Like songs, like weeping, those popular tunes from regions of South China told of the joys and the sorrows of life.

He played inside our house, sitting on his bamboo chair and crying since mother died. All the songs were about sadness and pain. Until one day, a neighbour came and asked him to stop.

He started to drink more and more.

The green bricks and green tiles of our house were also taken down piece by piece by creditors to repay debts. In the end, there was only one bedroom left and one bed. I no longer had a shelter for myself because I was the only girl. The beds of Sam Ma and my aunts were the places where I took turns to sleep. Sometimes I stayed in my mother's family home.

Sam Ma's bed contained wood fleas. I was often bitten, and couldn't sleep. Sam Ma would be unhappy while half asleep and half awake: 'May Oi, if you move around like a worm, I will kick you out of my bed.' I had to force myself to lay still and would wake with many red and itching spots on my body. I applied white flower oil on them. Then my aunts would tell me not to sit next to them and play mahjong because I smelt strongly of white flower oil—they couldn't bear it. Only when my aunt Sei Gu returned home did I have a chance to play mahjong.

'I like the smell of white flower oil,' she said. 'Come, May Oi, sit by me. Your smell can scare off the nasty mosquitoes around our feet.'

My kind aunt Sei Gu lived for one hundred and eight years.

Sam Ma was the daughter of a poor family. She came to our house when she was only twelve, and did the housework without pay; but had food and a bed. When she married my grandfather, she was already twenty-eight years old, an age already too old to find a man to marry. She was going to spend her life in the Hou home. In reality, she was just a woman sleeping in Grandfather's room at night and doing the same work during the day. After my grandfather passed away, the capable Sam Ma became the head of the household and managed all the affairs of the house. Though in fact, no one really regarded her as the new wife. My father included.

One day, Sam Ma delivered food to our home, and saw my father doing nothing, sitting on a chair with a pale and sad face looking at my mother's photo.

'You are the father of your three children, can you stand up like a responsible man?' she couldn't help but shout at him. 'Your wife would never have closed her eyes to her children missing their meals. What have you done? You only know how to cry, bang your head on the wall, and get drunk.'

My drunk father got up suddenly, grabbed a carrying pole from behind the door, and yelled at Sam Ma. His face became as red as his eyes. He held up the pole and was going to beat her. She ran out the door.

'You are a dead woman. Don't dare think you have the right to shout at me because you lie down on my old man's bed. You are only the servant!' My father yelled incoherently, chasing after her. The villagers ran out to watch the bustling and noise.

I followed my father and cried all the way; Gok trotted behind me, crying too; Kai was not crying—he kept calling out for our mother and followed us.

'God says even if she just crossed over your father's bed, she is still your mother to be respected. Such an ungrateful son—there will be retribution for beating your mother!' a woman neighbour said to me, grabbing me halfway.

Later, I heard that Sam Ma jumped into the waist-deep river and hid in the water plants under the bridge to escape my father's pursuit.

For the rest of my life, what the neighbour said that day has never been forgotten from the bottom of my heart. I always begged God: if there was to be retribution, please do it to me, not to my brothers or my sister.

4.4. Boarding a Red Boat

Every year, on the eighth day of the Chinese New Year celebrations, the villages always raised funds to invite the famous Cantonese opera troupe to come to the villages to perform a show. All shows were traditional stories of love, tragedy, or of a hero defending their homeland.

A temporary stage was built outside the ancestral hall. It was a great event for everyone in the village and the villages nearby. The festivities lasted for at least ten days, in order to bring good weather and a good life in the coming year.

That year it was the Yan Sau Nin troupe, one of the four largest troupes at that time. They performed *Charming Emperor*, a story of choosing love over riches and power, and *The Obstinate Princess and her Blunt Husband*, a story adapted from Shakespeare's *The Taming of the Shrew*. They were the Yan Sau Nin troupe's most famous shows.

The tamed princess says: 'If my husband asked, I would call the sun the moon, and the moon the sun.' That was my favourite line.

That night, I went home after a meal at Sam Ma's house. Home was a place with only ten square metres left. Under the faint kerosene lamp, I still could see the dark red satin quilt that was folded tidily inside the wooden bed. I could still see the large peony flower embroidered on it; the silk had begun to fray, but it was still beautiful. It was my mother's dowry.

My mother's large camphor trunk lay firm next to the bed. On top of it was a photo of my parents taken when they were in Hong Kong. It was a ceramic photo which sat on a carved dark wood stand. Father's erhu was lying beside, covered in dust. Gok and Kai were sitting together by the cooking fire stove at the end of the bed where embers still glowed, good for keeping them warm.

The only beautiful thing left in this house was a pretty green porcelain window on the top of the green brick wall.

Father was sitting on his broken-backed bamboo chair. On the small torn wooden table, his chipped china teacup was filled with tea.

'I am going to leave home to learn Cantonese opera,' I said, sitting on the bed.

Father looked at me, his grey lips moved, and he turned his head to reach out for the teacup and drank. I could hear the sound of him swallowing the tea.

'Is someone willing to accept you?' he asked.

'The master of the troupe. He said he could teach me to sing in a male voice style. He said my voice is suitable for this kind of role.'

'Oh, he is famous. Your mother and I used to watch him play.' Father took a sip of tea and swallowed it more loudly. He paused and asked, 'When are you going to be leaving?'

'Tomorrow. Tonight is their last play. They are moving on to Pan Yu.'

I looked at my shoes. This pair of beautiful red and black buttoned shoes were made with solid cloth. My mother had embroidered them with beads. At the time, she was pregnant with my sister sitting by the patio, stitching those red beads onto my shoes. She cocked her head and smiled slightly. Fortunately, my mother had bought me a bigger size, otherwise, even if I bent my toes while walking, my toe would have pierced through.

The lamp burner was flickering as I stood up and walked out the door. The cold wind blew right onto my face.

Sam Ma gave me a set of her old quilts and a torn leather suitcase which she had valued for many years.

'May Oi, we have sold almost all of our valuable things. There is no more left, really,' she sighed. 'I wish you learn your skills well, hope to be brilliant in the future, and bring pride to our ancestors one day.

Gok was already waiting for me outside the door the next morning.

'Sister, if you go, there will be no one washing our clothes,' he said between wiping his tears.

'I did teach you how to do it, you said you learned it.'

'I lied to you. I haven't learned it yet.'

I was holding back tears.

'Gok, I will write to you. I promise,' I said while trotting backwards.

Following behind the theatrical troupe I saw from a distance that Gok was following, then finally stopped. His right hand was waving.

I suddenly hesitated, and impulsively, almost turned back.

He was only eleven years old, I was thirteen.

If my father had said, 'Learn to be a troupe player? How dare you think of this choice?'

If Sam Ma had said, 'Stay at home, you will get what I get from the rice cylinder.'

If I had a matched future husband somewhere, waiting for me to grow up two more years.

Then that afternoon, I wouldn't have boarded a red boat with a golden dragon and chrysanthemum pattern, and left Heng Tin Village, my home.

The winter's river was even darker. Below deck, the only light was the flickering of flames from the river banks. I was lying down on the floor, right in the middle between sleeping people that I didn't know. I swore that I would study hard and learn how to fly over the walls with a bamboo pole just like the famous actress nicknamed 'Old Tangerine Skin Duck', the main actress in an all-girls Cantonese opera troupe. I liked her wit and style of humour. She was my idol.

Three years later, when I would return home to play a big show, everyone would praise me, 'May Oi, May Oi, our girl.'

Father would smile.

Sam Ma would be very busy greeting relatives and villagers who would come to visit.

Many people from my mother's family would also come to join us.

Everyone would be proud of me, and admire me.

4.5. Father Died

Just as the winter was ending and spring began, just over a year after I left home, my father had eaten watery congee with some chives and leek. He opened my mother's camphor trunk and took out three silver coins from the secret pocket in Mother's aqua-green satin gown.

'Gok, use them to buy some olives,' he said breathlessly. 'You can make pickled olives to sell. You must remember the little shop. It wasn't too far away from our home in Hong Kong.

I saw how they made them. He put the olives into a large wooden tube, added salt, and stepped on them until the olives softened, then he added five spice powder and liquorice and mixed it up well, leaving it for two days. You must learn to do it if we don't want to starve to death.'

'He said his chest was hurting again.' This was the description in Gok's letter written to me.

My father died in Gok's arms.

'All I could do was hold his body and cry,' Gok wrote. 'Kai didn't cry. He was sitting quietly on the bamboo stool.'

The letter was only a few lines, full of tears.

5. The Orphans

5.1. Pickled Airplane Olives

Most villagers had no shoes. Their bare feet would be toughened day after day by walking on the roads and fields, their soles becoming like a pair of hardened cow skin shoes. They could use them to walk everywhere. My brothers had grown these kind of shoes since our father died. Real shoes were to be saved for the bitter cold winter.

At night, with a paraffin lamp, Gok stood in a large wooden tub. His feet tread and tread on olives, both hands holding tightly onto the back of Father's bamboo chair. The olives became soft, and both of Gok's feet also became softer as well—the soles of his feet shoes had gone. This meant tomorrow Gok would have no shoes on. The little rocks on the road, the newly cut grass in the field, would be like sharp knives, cutting his feet, bleeding.

Gok would get up very early and cook rice congee with huge amounts of vegetables. Then he would wake up Kai. They would eat the first meal of a long day. The rest of the food was put into a metal tin, ready for their last meal at night.

Gok would put a large rooster-shaped bamboo-made basket on, strapped around his shoulders with the rooster head at the front, and the rooster tail at the back. Inside the rooster's body, there were at least four bags of pickled olives.

Eleven-year-old Gok and nine-year-old Kai were doing a little business as Father told them to sell pickled olives. They were called airplane olives because lots of customers in town would throw down money from balconies or windows, and the olives were thrown up to them, like flying airplanes. Gok would shout: 'Airplane olives, good taste, airplane olives, four for one penny!' He sometimes blew a small bamboo mouthpiece, playing a song to attract people's attention. Kai carried the metal congee tin following his older brother wherever he went, never leaving his sight.

The bamboo rooster wrapped Gok's small body as they walked from town to town, village to village. By the light of the moon they left home, by the light of the stars they came home, for more than three years.

5.2. Seeing Red

While my brothers struggled with life, I was a diligent and eager learner and worked hard to gain a better role in the troupe. I followed the red boat everywhere it went.

It was a stormy night. Thunder and lightning, wind and rain, folded together manically. The stage of a very wealthy family in Zhongshan was very grand. It was set in the middle of a lake and had an arched structure. It was well decorated with golden lacquer wood carvings. They paid good money to invite our troupe to perform in their home.

My master, who played Fa Dan, a main leading female role in Cantonese opera, was very happy and told us that everyone should work hard to avoid any disappointment of the host family, especially their most respected ninety-year-old mother.

Master's wife, who had the second leading male role, also took care of everything. She promised me she would instruct me especially to practice somersaults like a swallow, and she did, over the two years that had gone by.

She raised her hand and called me to come over as I practised in the garden. 'May Oi, it's rare for a master to value your potential. Don't let him down on his cultivation. I'll ask Yun to be your partner, she can practice with you.' She glanced at me and said again, 'The older you grow, the bigger your breasts will become. They are too heavy for you to do somersaults aren't they?' She turned me around. I didn't know why I wasn't growing much taller, but my breasts were growing so fast.

Yun was their youngest daughter, a few months younger than me. She was a good companion who was scared of her father's strictness.

The host family requested our troupe's speciality: *Dragon Tiger Crossing Jiang Gong*, a legendary ancient Chinese iconic tale, a story of love and power between humans and evil spirits and supernatural beings.

I liked the end: the main character paints a tiger on the ground, and the tiger comes alive; he rides on the tiger, flying into the sky, and disappears into the mist and clouds. That was the best part I liked most.

My role was a non-speaking one. I wrapped my breasts and was dressed as a man. I had a few somersaults, followed by a spear swing and another appearance. It was a small role that had been earned through two years of hard work.

The host family was very satisfied, and we performed five shows in a row. My master praised me for being good—my somersaults were neat enough. I was happy and proud. I swore in my heart that I would never forget my master's cultivation in the future.

That was the last play. Everyone was exhausted.

Heavy rain with thunder and lightning started just after the show ended. Finally, it stopped.

The sound of water was dripping from the eaves.

The cries of frogs, as one fell, and another one rose from the lake.

The snores came and went from people around me in the warehouse where we were sleeping.

I was deep asleep in the quilt that Sam Ma gave me.

Suddenly, a heavy and hot body with rapid breath, followed by a large hand pressing my mouth, a familiar smell of wax, a familiar face with two frantic eyes: 'Shh… shh… May Oi, it's me, just me—it will be quick, very quick.'

I pushed him away with one hand, and tightened my trousers with the other;

I bit his face with my teeth, he was bleeding;

I shouted to him—a beast;

His daughter woke up, only separated by a quilt;

His wife also woke up, only separated by two quilts;

Others were asleep on the grass hay lying on the ground—all woke up;

I was riding on the tiger's back, flying to the clouds.

In fact, I was like a corpse in his power.

I didn't even make a sound.

The fear that I never had in my life before, it was like it was happening in a nightmare where I wasn't able to call out a word.

I couldn't remember how long I was shivering.

The day dawned.

I put on my cotton coat and shoes and grabbed my things.

I saw Yun looking at me.

She wanted to say something, but she closed her eyes and turned her back to me.

I left.

All around was quiet. Not even a frog croak.

I took off my dirty trousers inside the bamboo groves by the road. I threw them into a nearby river.

I galloped to the town without shedding a single tear, but full of shame.

I was fifteen years and four months old.

On the last day of the Chinese New Year celebrations.

I became a woman who has seen red.

Two days later I arrived in Macau, on my father's cousin's doorstep. She was the only female who lived far away from home, and was kind to me when I was little. She was shocked to see me.

'I don't have a flair for opera,' I told her simply, and also begged her not to tell anyone in our family yet.

The troupe broke up later in June that year because they were deeply in debt. It disbanded since then.

I forget how many times in my life I have thought, if I were to meet my master again one day, I would use a little sharp knife to cut flesh piece by piece from his body, until he bled to death, begging for my mercy.

5.3. The Macau Boy Who Could Write Poems

I started to do a little business with my father's cousin's help. Every day I went to the fruit street stalls, looking for the best. I peeled them in a nice clean way, cut them into pieces, put them on a small plate and left them beside the opium beds next to those people in a haze, enfolded by opium.

When they ate the fruit, money would be left on the plate. Small money, but an income nonetheless. My days seemed promising in Macau.

Diagonally opposite the opium den, was Tiu's bakery. If my business was good, I would buy some of their steamed rice cakes, the soft glutinous rice stuffed with mashed green beans, salted egg yolks and fatty pork—almost the same as my Sam Ma's.

The pretty lady boss was always smiling. I called her Mrs Tiu. Sometimes I saw her son in the shop, who would write on the crimson rosewood table. He wore glasses and looked shy. When he saw me, he would get up and walk over to the counter to help his mother. Then, every time, I would see him waiting at the counter when I walked into the shop.

'May Oi, if you are late, my son Zung Man will cry,' his mother said one day. She also started to give me a few pieces of other desserts for free.

Life in Macau flew by so fast. My life seemed to start settling down. I decided to move out of my aunt's home. Mrs Tiu said, 'What a coincidence, I have a room. I won't charge you expensive rent, it is my luck to have you as my tenant really.'

I moved into their room on the third floor above the bakery shop, the same floor as Zung Man. The small living room between him and me became the place where he taught me poetry and writing.

One evening, Zung slipped a poem written with a fountain pen under the door of my room.

plum blossoms
beautiful as rain
love like rain
my heart is like a dream in mist
—Zung Man to May

The first feeling of love came smoothly.

As my aunt said, if my parents were still alive, they would have been happy too. It would be such a blessing to be married into a wealthy family if I was soon to be the young master's wife. I no longer went to the opium den to sell fruit. I put on a big apron and stood behind the counter of the bakery to greet customers. The customers said to his mother: 'Mrs Tiu, your future daughter-in-law is such a capable girl.' Zung would help me open the shop every day before going to school. He didn't talk much, but he wrote me a lot of beautiful poems.

Autumn was coming to Macau. Zung's father was going to celebrate his sixtieth birthday. 'You must go back to the hometown in Siu Hing to pay your respects and take May with you. It is time to introduce May to the family as well. I will stay in Macau to keep the shop open,' said Zung's mother.

Later I found out that Zung's mother was only a concubine. She couldn't actually be called 'Mrs Tiu' legitimately. The wealthy Tiu family owned hundreds of acres of fertile land and was a big landowner, owning nearly a whole street in the town. Zung's father had three wives and two concubines at the same time. Zung's mother was the only wife who lived outside their home, and Zung was the youngest of the Tiu family's six sons. They were wealthier than the Hou family.

The birthday celebration was to be held for three days and three nights and invited the most important people from ten miles around.

'Let us get out of here, I'll show you my town,' Zung said, coming into my room after breakfast. 'My father likes you, and my mothers are in the house.' He was happy, and so was I.

Outside the Tiu's large red main door, I stepped on the thick scattered remains of fireworks. They were burned red, laying ignored, and exuded the smell of gunpowder very strongly.

I saw a girl sitting on a wooden stool below the arcade of the grocery store just across the street. A long braid wrapped around her shoulders from the back; she was wearing a white floral Tang-style top, and she had wide black cloth trousers on with embroidered cloth shoes. She stared at me calmly. I thought maybe because I was wearing a slim-fitting *cheongsam* and leather shoes with heels, I was just being envied by this countryside girl.

The next morning —the third morning —I saw her still sitting on the same wooden stool, wearing the same set of clothes, with the same look.

'Do you know this girl? Is she your relative?' I asked Zung.

'No. I don't know her.' Zung didn't look at her. He took my hand and walked away.

After dinner in the evening, I went to the grocery store by myself.

'I want this cow bone comb please,' I said. I asked the boss, 'Where is your daughter, the one who is sitting outside every morning?

'She is not my daughter, but my wife's niece,' the boss said, taking a look at me. 'Don't you think poor people need to work? We are not like you—that lucky,' he sounded off snappishly.

'Who are you? Who are you to the Tiu's sixth young master? Or are you just one of *those* women from Macau?' the wife of the boss asked resentfully.

'My niece has been a child bride to the sixth young master since she was eight. She is his wife formally. Who are you? A concubine?' she mocked, her voice raising with anger. The wife tidied up the shelves which were already tidy.

'She should have married two years ago. It was supposed to be when she turned sixteen.'

The wife asked again, 'Who exactly are you?' She couldn't help but raise her voice.

The child bride tradition started during the Song Dynasty in China. These kinds of marriages occurred over a range of socio-economic classes but were particularly common among poor and rural families. Some of their daughters lived in their husbands' homes at an early age as a housemaid until they were old enough to marry, usually at the age of sixteen. Most of them were older than their husbands. The purpose was so the husband could be well looked after and the family had extra cheap labour. For those girls, they were always the 'married woman'. But the husbands were free to choose not to marry the child bride if they didn't want to (this tradition of arranged marriage was outlawed by the Communist Party after 1949).

Zung had a wife—he wasn't being honest with me. I didn't want to be a concubine despite the chance for me to have a decent home.

That night, I left Siu Hing, and took a boat to Hong Kong. I did not say goodbye to Zung.

The sea in the night was like a boundless sky. I couldn't see what was ahead of me. My father's oldest brother was my last hope.

Zung and I have never seen each other since. But I never forgot his poems, and felt grateful for what he taught me.

6. Meeting Them in the War

6.1. Japanese Coming to Hong Kong

It was 1937, the year that the Marco Polo Bridge incident happened. I was eighteen. I was doing my little business, which was the same kind as in Macau. But, I was selling fresh fruits in the street instead. I was doing well. I got my own place to sleep. I shared a room with a girl called Miss Keung. She had a foreign name: Pauline.

One year before, I left Zung and arrived in Hong Kong in the morning. The moment I bent my head down and walked out of the dilapidated cabin—the smell of the place was so familiar: the air permeated an ocean flavour, slightly fishy and sweaty; and also tobacco; the sweetness of the steamed rice cupcake with red beans, *Put Chai Ko*; the aroma of the fresh fried chestnuts…

It took me almost an hour to walk to my father's oldest brother's home on Nathan Road, the same road our family home was on years ago. There it was, still a flour and rice shop, but now owned by someone else.

Outside of my uncle's dry seafood shop, I saw a young man serving customers. He greeted guests with a humble smile on his face. He was my oldest cousin.

'Miss, what are you looking to buy? Our dried shrimp are the best all over the city. They just arrived yesterday. Come, take a look,' he asked attentively, when he saw me walking in.

'I am May Oi—don't you recognise me, cousin?' I said with a deep sigh of relief.

'Heh, heh, no wonder you looked familiar to me. Can't believe you are a big girl now,' he said politely. 'Come in and have a cup of tea. I thought you were in Macau.'

I was thirsty and hungry. I put down the suitcase and drank a big cup of hot tea. My cousin kept himself busy the whole time, even with no customers.

'It's hard to do business, if only enough for two meals,' he sighed and shook his head.

'Is Uncle at home?' I asked. I was wishing to see my oldest uncle.

'Oh, my father is taking a nap. It's not good to wake him up. He is old now. You know.'

I got up to say goodbye and choked back my tears.

'You are free to come anytime, May Oi.' My cousin followed me out. He didn't ask where I was going to stay that night.

They were the only relatives I had in Hong Kong. My uncle was the father figure in the family and was in charge of major events after my grandfather passed away. I thought I could rely on them for a short while, at least to have a meal and bed on my first day back in Hong Kong.

I haven't heard from them since. I felt I was abandoned by my family. I felt I was disliked for being bad. I began to tell people I was from the North; that my surname was 'Gam'; that my name was 'May', one word only. May.

I sometimes deliberately passed by our old home and my uncle's shop. From across the road, I could see my cousin was busy, and occasionally saw my old uncle lying on a larger bamboo chair at the arcade, waving a big palm-leaf fan. He looked so much like my grandfather.

Many times I wanted to talk to them and tell them how I had been and what I was doing. But I didn't have any kind of honourable things to tell them. Moreover, I was ashamed to go back to our root village home to worship ancestors and see Sam Ma. I was always in tears and often couldn't control them. I was ashamed of myself.

6.2. A Wealthy Hong Kong Boy

At that time, everyone in Hong Kong was cheering for the motherland to fight against Japan. 'Only patriotism can save the country, and failure to resist will lead to destruction.' The young waved flags and shouted as loud as they could in the street. People burned with indignation. They handed out leaflets. They played dramas in street performances to denounce the crimes of the Japanese and sang of the fighters' brave deeds. The attitude of the neutral state Britain, made Hong Kong the only channel for foreign aid to enter China. It was the most important channel during that period. The big companies that moved to Hong Kong from the mainland to escape the Japanese, even banks, became suppliers of anti-Japanese war materials. Yes—they made a fortune at the same time.

July 7th 1938, was the first anniversary of the Marco Polo Bridge Incident. In July 1937, a battle between China's National Revolutionary Army and the Imperial Japanese Army started over the excuse of a missing Japanese soldier. It is generally regarded as the start of the Second Sino-Japanese War. The Japanese invasion of China turned into a full-scale occupation and was also regarded as the beginning of World War II in Asia.

Across industries in Hong Kong, large fundraising activities were held to support China's fight against Japan. All merchants in Hong Kong donated one day's business; the famous Cantonese opera actors donated all ticket sales.

On that day, I put all the money from my pockets, and all my gold and silver jewellery into the donation box.

'Miss, your actions are very touching,' a handsome student stepped forward and said to me.

'Compatriots, it is everyone's responsibility to fight against Japan and save the nation. If this lady can do it, we can all do it,' he called out loudly to the people around him.

'Miss, we have a meeting tomorrow, can you come to attend? One more person adds one more strength.'

He had bright eyes with sincere brilliance, a clean face, and neatly waxed hair.

'Okay,' I agreed decisively.

This young man's name was Sang from Wah Yan College Hong Kong. A famous private boys school, it was the first English-language school run by the Chinese-Christian Society of Hong Kong.

I became a member of their performance team for anti-Japanese National Salvation. Two years of training in a troupe was useful. On the busy street, whenever I sang in my male-style voice: 'Killing the enemy with my ambitious heart'—with one kick and one hand slash, my heroic movements and indignant face brought rapturous applause every time. Sang was always the one who clapped wildly and cheered loudly.

Later, because the then Hong Kong Governor Sir Geoffrey Alexander Stafford was under the threat of pressure from the Japanese and was afraid of their anger and afraid they would be beaten, he started up a new department called the Chinese Newspaper Inspection Office, which specifically edited anti-Japanese slogans they thought were too radical.

Our team decided to print its own newspapers. Sang was the main writer. He and his friends walked through the small streets and delivered their newspapers. I often left my fruit stall early and walked with him to deliver newspapers and leaflets. We met the student representative from England, Bernard Fried. I heard him passionately read two public statements from the World Federation of Young Students:

> *Declaration to aid Chinese Students in the Struggle to Report to Students All Over the World.*
>
> *Resolution of the World Student Congress on Aid to Chinese Students' Struggle.*

Sang patted me on the shoulder very enthusiastically, forgetting that I couldn't understand a word. 'May, what exciting news,' he said. 'I'll translate it into Chinese for you tomorrow.'

On the second night, Sang came to my flat and gave me the Chinese version of the open letter neatly written in fountain pen, and asked me out.

'May, a new movie *Blood Splattered Baoshan City* has just arrived in cinemas. Will you watch it with me?' he asked.

It was a true story of Chinese soldiers who vowed to live and die in Baoshan city. They repelled the Japanese attacks many times, until they all sacrificed their lives. It demonstrated the noble national integrity and sacrificial spirit of Chinese anti-Japanese fighters—a tragic and exciting national march. We stood up a few times in the middle of the movie and clapped and shouted, our hearts afire, just like everyone else in the cinema, nothing more.

My brother Gok also joined the army of the Nationalist Party of Chiang Kai-shek on the mainland. It wasn't due to his willingness. He was forced to join by the government policy despite him being younger than sixteen years old.

'I thought because I was much smaller than my age, they wouldn't put their eyes on me,' Gok wrote in a letter. 'If I was smart enough that day, I wouldn't have been caught, and Kai wouldn't have been left alone.'

Gok had to leave home three days later. Kai was standing at the door again, motionless, with no goodbyes, no tears, no words. He kept his head down, staring at his new pair of shoes his brother bought him with his first advanced pay as a soldier. Gok comforted him and promised he would be back soon and now they didn't need to sell pickled olives anymore. He would bring money home.

Kai was left at home alone for nearly a year until our mother's brother took him to Guangzhou and found him a tailor apprenticeship, with no pay, but a place to sleep, and rice in his bowl. He started his tailoring life at age twelve.

One day, I had just got home. Pauline was cooking in the kitchen which we shared with other tenants. 'You will see Sang's mother if you come back early,' said Pauline, putting down the grilled red snapper on the table. 'She was looking for you. She wants to see what kind of girl you are. She is rich, May.' Those who get into prestigious schools, of course, their families must be rich. Pauline continued to talk as she went back to the kitchen stir-frying the pak choi with garlic.

'She said that you have a mango-like face, not as pretty as how her son described you.' Pauline turned over the pak choi, the smell of garlic filling the whole third floor of the old building. 'If I knew she was going to look at your photo, I would have taken it down from the wall.'

I took a closer look at the photo hanging on the wall. Compared to Pauline, sitting beside me in the photo, my face did look a bit like a mango shape.

'What else did she say?' I asked, going into the kitchen anxiously.

'She said her son is planning not to go to school anymore. He is going to start his own business instead, earn money to support a girl named May. He doesn't want to depend on his family.'

Pauline put down the well-cooked pak choi, and headed back to the kitchen again. 'The fatty large fish intestines with the bitter grapefruit peel mixed so well. Can't throw them away,' Pauline said, 'I heated them up.'

'They are from two days ago Pauline,' I said.

'May, I must say, Sang's mother isn't an easy woman. She looked like a most demanding mother-in-law.' Pauline put down her chopsticks. 'A big jade, gold earrings, a ruby ring, a pair of shiny leather shoes, and a silk-made *cheongsam*. After speaking for a while, she stepped downstairs, got into a rickshaw which was waiting on the street and swaggered off. I saw from the balcony.'

I ate silently. I had no words.

'May, we are sworn sisters. I'm the elder. I must advise you that those students are really making trouble for themselves: you should not be one of them. Who is Sang, and who are you? You don't even dare admit that you are surnamed Hou. Besides, I am the only person who knows you are not surnamed Gam—who else knows? It's not that you don't understand that bamboo doors should match bamboo doors, and wooden doors should match wooden doors…' Pauline stopped and sighed. 'You don't need me to tell you, you know what I mean.'

That night, I stared at the top of the mosquito net and stayed up all night. Pauline was right, how could I be good enough for him? What do I do to be worthy of him?

I had no family in Hong Kong. I didn't even dare to tell anyone my real last name. I wouldn't make the family cheer on the wedding night to see the red.

I decided not to join the performance team anymore, not to see Sang again. My fruit stall had also changed places.

But Sang would find his way to see me. He was always around me.

6.3. My Sister-Like Friend, Pauline

My dearest friend Pauline, was three years older than me. We were the same people who fell from the ends of the world; we became friends who shared our secrets, almost everything. We promised each other that we would be sisters till the end of our lives.

We rented a room and shared the rent. Moreover, she was at home every day, so she could cook. After I closed my fruit stall, I bought food on my way home.

Pauline came to Hong Kong with her grandaunt from a small village in Guangdong when she was ten years old. 'Until my mother's aunt came from Hong Kong to visit us on the new year, I didn't know what proper shoes looked like,' Pauline told me. 'I begged her to take me with her, and my parents too.'

As Pauline was the middle of six children, her father was going to throw her in a large wooden pail of urine when she was born a girl. 'My grandmother saved me. She said I may get married to a good family and bring fortune to us. I was fed with rice-cooked soup. My grandmother often carried me on her back walking to different houses, begging for milk.'

Pauline came to Hong Kong, as she wished, and got a pair of shoes. She became her grandaunt's adopted daughter. This meant she needed to look after her grandaunt when she was old and sick. She learned from her grandaunt how to make laundry detergent. For years she was shouted at and beaten until her laundry skills were even better than her grandaunt. Clothes ironed and starched by Pauline wouldn't wrinkle for three months.

Every morning, Pauline put on a bamboo pole, and on each side was a large empty bamboo basket. She went to the naval vessels in Wan Chai to collect dirty clothes from the soldiers. She would be very happy if her baskets were full of them.

Pauline soaped the dirty clothes in two big wooden basins beside the well in the backstreet, left them for a while on a slate, and then scrubbed them on a wooden board vigorously. Before lunch Pauline needed to have finished all the washing; she then had to move them back home, put them into a big pot, starch and stir them carefully with a wooden stick; then after that, she carried them back to the well and rinsed them with water.

Every day Pauline begged for a sunny day, so her clothes could be dried on the rooftop. After dinner, I washed the dishes, and Pauline started ironing.

In winter, Pauline's hands and feet were cracked a lot and bleeding, it was very painful.

Sixteen-year-old Pauline became pregnant by a Canadian soldier whom she knew from the military base. It was he who gave her a foreign name: Pauline.

Her grandaunt flew into a rage for her niece being such a disgrace and for bringing shame to her and the family. She didn't give her food, didn't give her money, and tried to force her to have an abortion. But Pauline was determined to give birth.

'I bought a lot of baby clothes secretly, and hid them at the bottom of the closet. My aunt found out and cut them to pieces, one by one,' Pauline told me one night.

'My grandaunt scolded me every day and beat me almost every day over any excuse. I thought she was hoping for me to miscarry. Luckily my baby stuck around in my stomach till he was born.' When Pauline returned home from the maternity home called The Seventh Aunt, on Middle Ring road, run by the self-taught woman 'Picking Mama', her grandaunt refused to let them in. Pauline was hugging her son kneeling outside her home, begging her grandaunt. She was in the cold wind for hours.

'My son was a very handsome boy, May,' Pauline started happily from her bed, 'You know, May, he had a high nose bridge and blue eyes—he looked like a pilot. I fed him so well, my milk was just like a fountain. He grew up so fast, in only three months he could sit up, and in six months, stand up.'

But the Canadian soldier didn't accept the fact he was the father. He even disappeared soon after. No one was willing to tell her where he had gone.

'My baby was much like a westerner, he often laughed like his father,' said Pauline.

I had never met Pauline's son.

'He was fine that day. He ate a big bowl of lean pork congee in the afternoon. At midnight, I found him burning up. He couldn't even cry.'

'Why didn't you take him to see the doctor?' I asked.

'My grandaunt said that a child will grow up quickly when he has a fever, there was no need to make a fuss. She said to wait till dawn to see if his fever didn't go away. I held him in my arms and waited,' Pauline told me.

The next morning, Pauline's pilot was out of breath. He was only one year old.

'It must be his fate. So easy to die. Only a fever,' Pauline's grandaunt said.

Pauline wrapped her son up in his quilt and buried her little pilot on the mountain. A wooden board was erected on a small round-shaped mound. There were no words written on it, because Pauline couldn't write.

She drew a cross on the wooden board; 'Like that word on the top of the church,' she explained.

Not long after her son's death, Pauline moved out of her grandaunt's home and rented a bedsit.

'The next day, and every day since, I got up early, and went to the military camp to fetch all their dirty clothes before my grandaunt went,' Pauline smiled indulgently as she told me.

'She lost her business eventually, and went back to her countryside village home in mainland China.'

One morning, Pauline got up and looked terrified. 'May, I saw my grandaunt standing in front of my bed last night, it was in the middle of the night. She even opened the mosquito net and looked straight at me. She looked very nasty.'

'Just a dream, Pauline. I didn't see anyone last night, I only heard you snoring,' I laughed.

A month later, Pauline received a letter from her village home. I read it for her. It said that her grandaunt had passed away a month ago. The same day Pauline saw her at night.

6.4. Meeting Andrew

The Japanese were getting closer and closer to Hong Kong as the mainland lost cities one by one. But in Hong Kong it seemed that there was no sense of danger, everyone's days were as usual.

In Gok's letter sent from the mainland, he told me he spent most of his time training for fighting. But he hadn't met a single Japanese yet. He was glad about that because he was the smallest person on his team. He would have been the first person to be shot by the Japanese, because he had been bullied, and was warned that he would be on the front line on the battlefield. But he did fire a gun a few times into the trees.

The good thing was he had food. 'I must fill the rice tin half-full first, eat quickly, then go back to get a full tin. If not, the big wooden barrel of rice will be empty,' said Gok proudly. He also astonished me: he learned how to sleep while walking.

In Hong Kong, more and more soldiers were seen on the streets. Bars and clubs had become places where most of them had fun on the weekends. Some people also liked to go to the rollerskating rink, like me.

I was a good skater. I was like a swallow through the crowd; I could circle on one leg, and jump on both feet, my floral dress flying with me.

I noticed that there was always a pair of eyes following me outside the fence: he was wearing a British uniform with three bars on his sleeve. He was tall.

One day, at the encouragement of his friend, he was trembling as he skated, and stumbled against the railing.

I flew lightly beside him several times.

His fair and innocent face smiled; I could see the honest expression in his blue eyes.

'Come on, be a man.' Suddenly, a few of his friends pushed him from behind toward me. He fell hard. Poor him, he was still struggling on the ground trying to get up when I skated around back to him, and his friends laughed outrageously.

'Come,' I reached out to him, laughing.

This six-foot tall young man's name was Andrew Clark Devlin, from Scotland's capital, Edinburgh. A place I had never heard about.

Along with the other new young soldiers, he shipped to Hong Kong ten months before from Edinburgh and belonged to the Royal Regiment of Scotland. As the senior and only Scottish line infantry of the British Army Infantry, it was one of the main forces of the British defenders of Hong Kong in World War II.

Andrew started to invite me to go out. 'My home, Edinburgh, is a city smaller than Hong Kong; the rocky roads either go uphill or downhill similar to Hong Kong. Not easy to walk if you wear high heels like you. However, it is a really special city with the elegance of Queen Elizabeth, and also the liveliness and the prettiness of her two daughters.' That was how Andrew described Edinburgh to me. He showed me a photo of the King's family.

'The girls are not smiling. Especially the older one,' I said.

'I think they must be stressed out by the photographer,' Andrew laughed.

I never thought that one day I would meet the older daughter—Queen Elizabeth II.

Most times Andrew and I went to the cinema to watch movies or danced in the club. I bought a dictionary to learn English and I bought a pair of high heel shoes to be able to reach his shoulder height. I made a few dresses because he told me that I looked beautiful in a dress.

One night, just after we left the cinema, an American military jeep suddenly lost control and turned over in the middle of the road. While everyone was shocked and dumbfounded, including me, Andrew had already rushed over.

He grabbed the driver out, then the passenger who was bleeding from his face. The petrol was leaking—a fire could happen any minute. The crowd gaped in awe.

I felt proud of him when people around me said, 'This *gweilo* was so fast, he is a very brave soldier.' Some people even gave a thumbs up in front of us.

That night, I told Pauline that I was going to marry this *gweilo*. 'He is too tall for you,' Pauline said in surprise. 'As a soldier, the Japanese are coming—aren't you afraid that he will be killed? You are going to be a widow.'

'He is a kind man, honest and well-behaved. And his neat handwriting is like print—he must have been to a good school, he was well educated.'

'Do you know how to read English writing, which looks like chicken intestines? You and him are just like chickens talking to ducks, it won't make sense,' Pauline shook her head.

'Then what about your son's father?' I asked scornfully.

'...But he was not tall and matched me very well. I was too young, I didn't understand anything. I thought he really liked me and would take me away from my grandaunt to Canada. How could I know he was just fooling me? Come to think of it, I felt so stupid and so naive to believe in him. He ruined my life, you know?' Pauline cried and added, 'Do you want yourself like me, May?'

'Pauline, what chance do we have to marry a Chinese man? We don't even have a home, we don't have family. We don't have anyone to talk to about such things around a marriage, like the day, the wedding gift money, the rites, the... We are not as we should be... As a girl.'

We were both speechless.

'We are getting older every year. Do you want to be an old girl? People will gossip that something is wrong with us. We are the leftover girls.' I was telling her the truth that I couldn't help but worry about.

I lay down, staring at the top of the mosquito net. Pauline blew out the kerosene lamp on the table between us. This lamp was used after dinner because she insisted on not using the electric light to save money.

Pauline let out a long sigh. 'You're right, maybe, May. Last time our block had a fire, we don't even know how your *gweilo* boyfriend knew about it. He rushed upstairs and even moved my things down,' Pauline said. 'At least you won't be afraid of being bullied while you have a tall *gweilo* beside you, and people would show you more respect. I think, for me, no more *gweilo*. Mostly, I will just be on my own, I am not going to marry anyone. Who wants me? A plain woman who has given birth without marriage.' Pauline tried to appear casual, but I could hear the regret in her voice.

'At least this *gweilo* has only one wife, no concubines,' I said, 'I'll take my chance.'

Pauline didn't answer. I was sure she was pretending to be asleep.

6.5. I Proposed

On a beautiful sunny Sunday, on April 27th 1941, I was going to marry nineteen-year-old Andrew Devlin. The fortune teller on the corner said this day was a good day for marriage, and also for making fortunes and sacrifices to ancestors. It seemed a perfect day.

'Sunday is perfect, all my friends can join us.' Andrew was happy too.

It was just six weeks before, another movie weekend. Andrew and I watched the movies *Citizen Kane* and *Suspicion* at the Lee Theatre in Causeway Bay.

We got on the last tram back to my home. I looked at Andrew, who was holding my hand, gathered up all my courage and said: 'Are we getting married?'

What I saw was surprise and thrill in Andrew's eyes. '...Yes, we are going to marry, May, yes. When?' Andrew clasped my two hands to his chest, I could feel his heart beating faster.

Then—on that Sunday morning.

I was sat in my room looking in the mirror. I dabbed on foundation, brushed my delicately shaved eyebrows, shaped with a string like my mother's, and put on a bright lipstick.

That makeup set was Max Factor, it was my first gift from Andrew. He bought it in the most luxurious superstore, Lane Crawford, a British store that sold everything. Most customers were Western and some were wealthy Chinese. Since then, I used no other brands. Always Max Factor.

Pauline combed my hair slowly from the top to the end. 'One comb, comb to the end; two combs, till white hair to the eyebrows; three combs, children and grandchildren everywhere,' she said.

Combing a bride's hair was tradition. People believed it was a very important step on the wedding day, it would affect the bride's future married life. When my aunts married, their mother chose the happiest woman in the village to comb her daughter's hair, hoping it would bring lifelong happiness to them. Pauline certainly wasn't the happiest woman but she was the only person like family I had in Hong Kong. The room we shared was my home and from there, from that day, I would become a 'Mrs'.

The elegant noble black and gold Rolls-Royce came and waited on the street. All the neighbours rushed out to watch. Everyone was so envious of me when I walked down from the second floor.

In the spring breeze, my veil was fluttering, as if a happily dancing little angel came and went across my face. I was smiling.

Looking up at the sky, I hoped my mother was looking down at me with her sweetest smile. 'May Oi, my girl, your hair is so neatly combed; your eyebrows are so well-shaven like a crescent moon.'

I wanted to tell her: 'Mother, I bought my camphor wood trunk from that Ming Dynasty redwood furniture store on Newton Road where we have been before. It is beautiful like yours, just a little bigger, because I am going carry many things to places where you and I have never been.'

The Rolls-Royce stopped outside the Cathedral of the Immaculate Conception on Caine Road, Hong Kong Island. Andrew was in his smart uniform and stood on the other end of the red carpet with his uniformed comrades.

Andrew was so hurried when he saw me getting out of the car that he forgot the ground under his feet and almost fell. Everyone laughed.

A faint aroma came from the white lily of the valley I held in my hand which I had chosen. '*Happiness with luck coming, finally, from far away*'—I believed what the flower shop owner told me. My white wedding dress had a long train, trailing on the red floor and covering my white six-inch high-heeled shoes. I walked slowly towards Andrew, alone, to the man I was prepared to spend the rest of my life with—a foreigner whom I had only known for six months.

'*This girl is going to marry far, far away, sailing across the sea.*' Just like the prophecy of the blind woman. She was telling the truth. I wondered, how did she see through me? How could I not believe it?

My name now was Doris, named by Andrew.

He liked the song *My Dreams Are Getting Better All The Time* sung by Doris Day, an American actress and singer. He also said that my face shape was a little like hers. 'You don't know how beautiful you are, May, just like Doris Day,' said Andrew on the dance floor one night.

There was a crucifix above the altar.

'I, Andrew Owen Devlin, take you, Doris Hou May to be my wife. I promise to be true to you in good times and in bad, in sickness and in health. To love you and honour you all the days of my life.' Andrew's hand was shaking, his right hand on his left chest.

'I, Doris Hou May, take you, Andrew Owen Devlin, to be my husband. I promise to be true to you in good times and in bad, in sickness and in health. To love you and honour you all the days of my life.'

Andrew was smiling, he was so relieved that his days spent teaching me to speak those words in English had just gone very well.

I was glad that he hadn't forgotten to bring those rings. I chose and paid for them. They were thick and square, lying quietly on the white silk cushion.

Andrew put the ring on my finger.

I had my tears running down.

The ring has never been taken off my finger since that beautiful day in Hong Kong. Its square shape has become a rounded line over the years.

For the first time, I officially wrote down my surname as 'Hou', and my birthplace as Heng Tin Village of Namhoi, Guangdong. I no longer claimed my surname was 'Gam' and that I came from the north. I had myself confirmed as a Catholic.

My family was Buddhist, worshipping Guanyin, or 'Gun Yam' in Cantonese. There were always some incense sticks burning in my home from as early as I could remember. Wherever I lived, there was always a figure of merciful Gun Yam in the house with fresh chrysanthemum and fresh fruit alongside it. Gun Yam's appearance was dignified and kind and held a clean bottle of willows. We believed in Gun Yam's wisdom and great magical power, as well as in their infinite compassion and mercy—they could save us from disaster as long as we recited their name. Now, for a *gweilo*, I needed to give Gun Yam up.

I burned a stick of incense, praying and begging for his or her blessing and protection before I walked out of my home in my wedding dress—this was the last Gun Yam shrine in my home.

It was so important to hear what the Cantonese-speaking priest told me: 'Catholics are encouraged to marry other Catholics and can attain a perfect union of mind and full communication of life.' The priest explained to me at Andrew's request, 'I am the priest on the day assigned to commemorate your marriage as part of God's natural law and to support you two if you and Andrew do choose to marry.'

Even more important was to know that Andrew was an unmarried man and didn't have a marriage contract with anybody in his home, Edinburgh.

God will bless me and Andrew and our children and my brothers always. I believed and felt protected. I took my marriage vows and would keep them. No matter what, I swore to myself.

In a letter to my brother Gok, I wrote: '…I am going to get married. He is a British soldier from Scotland, and like you, a soldier. And he can write well, like you too. Soon you and Kai can come to Hong Kong to be with me.'

Gok replied: 'My sister, I bought a large English dictionary at the bookstore yesterday, and I will bring it to Hong Kong for you. I also bought a pocket-sized copy myself. I can learn English when I have time.'

Before long, I received a pair of silk pillowcases with embroidered phoenixes and dragons from Guangzhou—it was very nice satin silk, sent by Gok.

In a small flat with a tiny living room in a two-storey building in North Point, sharing a kitchen and bathroom with another family, my life started as Mrs Doris Hou May Devlin at my actual age, twenty-one. But on my marriage certificate, I was nineteen, the same age as Andrew. The day and the month of birth were just my guess, because I couldn't remember, and no one could tell me. I chose the same year as Andrew; the day and month I chose to be near the end of October, the 26th. Autumn in Hong Kong is the cosy season.

I didn't tell him I wasn't a virgin.

And I never have told him.

The 'red' had been taken before him.

I liked when Andrew called me 'darling' the next morning with his shying sweet smile after we spent our first night together. I liked it very much.

7. Japanese Singing in Hong Kong

7.1. Hong Kong in Pain

That morning, it was cold and overcast. I took a trolley bus and walked to Pauline's home. Pauline was cooking pure rice congee. She yelled from the kitchen, 'May, go get some deep-fried bread sticks—they must be from the one on the corner!'

I knew she meant the one owned by a young couple, Mr and Mrs Ho, just on the left side on the corner of the street. They made the best bread sticks—crispy on the outside and soft on the inside, full of southern beancurd cheese flavour.

In summer, I could see the wife swinging a large palm leaf behind her husband while he was sweating profusely. They smiled at me every time I passed by.

'Good morning. How many do you want today?' Mrs Ho asked, with a sweet and girlish voice. I liked her voice very much.

'What a waste if you don't sing in the Cantonese opera—you would be very popular,' I said to her once. I thought she was suitable for the role of the Wealthy Miss in the opera.

They were a hard-working couple. They got up early and returned home late to make a living. Their daughter sat in the bamboo highchair on the other side of the road.

She was wearing a pink cotton-padded jacket and a cute lion head hat which I saw Mrs Ho knit, not long ago. It was similar to the one I knitted for my long-lost little sister.

This beautiful two-year-old was laughing, playing a drum in her little hands. I was wondering why Mrs Ho left her daughter over there—she probably wanted her to be a bit further away from the burning smoke when they deep-fried the bread in fat oil.

It was December 8th 1941, morning, about eight o'clock. After breakfast, I was just sitting down with Pauline and two other girls who were from next door. We were going to carry on the mahjong game we had left the night before.

Suddenly the air siren rang out harshly. Pauline joked, 'Again? Have they got nothing to do?' One of the girls said, 'I am not scared. My cousin said we have strong allied armies who come from Canada, India, and China. My cousin trains himself on how to fight every day. He is ready to die for Hong Kong. How silly he is.'

At that time a lot of Hong Kong people were on fire with zeal to defend their native lands—especially the young. Sang certainly was one of them. He was one of fifteen young Chinese men who joined the Royal Hong Kong Regiment and had received artillery training.

But to most Hong Kong residents and the British, the threat from Japan seemed far away. Watching movies, plays in the theatre, football and horse racing, dancing, drinking, shopping—life went on as usual in Hong Kong. They believed if the Japanese came, the British troops should have enough power to defeat the enemy.

The newspapers told us Hong Kong was the last fortress of defence, it was the South China doorway; Great Britain was very concerned about Hong Kong's role in the world. Even Minister Churchill once said although Hong Kong can't stick to it, it must be defended. In reality, Hong Kong was surrounded by the enemy; Britain was very over-confident.

I knew Hong Kong would not be protected. Hong Kong was on its own. Because two months before 8th December 1941, Andrew was transferred to India with his commander. We were just six months married. He was the general's clerk and was promoted two levels higher in a row quickly because the general's clerk must be of Sergeant rank. The rest of his team stayed in Hong Kong to defend against incoming Japanese troops. If the Japanese attacked Hong Kong, how could we win the battle if the general was not even there? But I was still hoping, naively.

And, I just had an unexpected miscarriage. It happened on that last Sunday morning before Andrew left Hong Kong: we found blood everywhere on our bed. I thought I was having a period. I rushed to the toilet, and a big piece of bloody ball came out of me. I knew something wasn't right.

'You have miscarried,' we were told by a doctor in hospital. We were shocked.

'Darling, a baby will come again, as many as we want,' Andrew comforted me. But I began to think that it could have been caused by my sins. My body wasn't clean. It had been invaded by the devil and my womb was stained filthy, a good baby won't grow up there. That thought, like a shadow, lived in my mind.

Before Andrew left home, I cooked a pot of rice congee for the last meal. I filled it into a large bowl, added two tablespoons of sugar and stirred it well.

Andrew couldn't eat rice. The first time he ate it, he almost vomited it out. Seeing him try so hard to swallow every day was funny, and I felt sorry for him. I found a solution which was 'sweet rice': I served my bowl first, and then put sugar in the rest. Andrew happily called it rice pudding. Since then, my *gweilo* husband fell in love with rice.

'Darling, I don't want to go. You know that, don't you?' Andrew said.

'But you have to, don't you? I can manage myself, you must not worry about me.' I picked up a nice piece of char siu and put it down in his sweet rice. This roast pork was his favourite Chinese dish, it was one of my specialities.

'Darling, war is coming.' Andrew looked into my eyes and gave me a little new red book—it was a bank book. 'Here are all my savings. I just saved them in Shanghai Bank with both our names. You must use it, darling.'

It was a few hundred, a huge amount of money at that time.

'Don't forget, you insisted on paying most of our wedding costs, including our rings. I am not as poor as you think us soldiers are,' Andrew said with a cheeky smile.

That night we both couldn't sleep. 'When the war is over, either we have our home in Hong Kong—I like Hong Kong—or you come to Edinburgh. My family are going to love you, I am so sure of that. Particularly my sisters,' Andrew said. 'First, we will have a girl, who looks like you, second, a boy, who looks like me; then another girl who looks like the both of us. Darling, what do you think?'

We promised each other that no matter what happened, we would do our best to stay alive, and the words we vowed to each other at church would hold. I put my hand on my left chest as he did on our wedding day. Then we cried when the daybreak came.

7.2. The Horrors of the Air Raid

It was only at the start of the third round of the mahjong game when we heard faint rumbling from the distance.

'Stop mixing the mahjong tiles,' I said.

A terrible roaring sound was coming closer and closer: it was the sound of real airplanes, they seemed to be just above our heads.

In a second, in a deafening noise, everything shook and collapsed in dust. We all screamed and cried. We ran out the half-hanging door and found the staircase from the first floor to the ground floor had collapsed.

I shouted, 'Go up, go up!'

The girls followed me with the other terrified people.

Pauline dragged on my cardigan hem right behind me.

We went up to the rooftop and climbed over the fence to the next building.

My hands were badly hurt when I grabbed a rose plant.

I noticed Pauline only had one clog on her left foot. Her bare right foot was bleeding.

'May, we are going to die, going to die. I know it,' Pauline was convulsing with fear and kept saying words she didn't mean to.

Outside the street were horrible scenes that have haunted me for the rest of my life.

We didn't know where was safe.

I just ran with my pair of clogs and followed those terrified people.

I saw Mr and Mrs Ho's stall disappear along with the whole block.

Their daughter was still sitting inside the bamboo high chair; her cries broke into a violent lament, her hat gone: she had been covered up with thick dust.

I rushed to take her out and carried her on my back.

I knew the nearest air raid shelter was just a few blocks away. I needed to get there before all those other people running to the same place.

That was the fastest I ran in my life. When I finally got there, I saw Pauline was already inside. She must have left me when I stopped to get the little girl out.

We all realised the Japanese had come, and the war had started for real.

After eighteen days of death and bloody battles in Hong Kong, on the 25th December 1941 in the afternoon, the British Governor Sir Mark Aitchison Young was surrounded in person in the Japanese headquarters on the third floor, Room 336 of The Peninsula Hotel.

I always thought this poor man must have been very humiliated when he carried a white flag walking alongside Queen's Road. I also thought that the Japanese wanted the British colony of Hong Kong to remember her humiliation on the most celebrated day, forever.

That day has been called 'Hong Kong's Black Christmas' ever since.

Before that morning of Christmas Day, Japanese infantry took control of the remaining water reservoirs and the power station.

Before that morning, troops were killed in Repulse Bay.

Before that morning, the Japanese entered the British Field Hospital at St. Stephen's College and killed 150 wounded soldiers. Three British and four Chinese nurses were raped and murdered. There was no more resistance by the dwindling garrison forces. Major General Christopher Maltby said afterwards if they had not surrendered then, there would have been more innocent killed.

Years later, I found out Hong Kong never had a chance to win this battle. Nearly one Hong Kong soldier fought for every four Japanese on the ground; forty-seven Japanese Air Self-Defence Force were in the sky, but only five RAF airplanes, which were destroyed in the first hours. Hong Kong troops seriously lacked battle strength and combat experience.

Japanese troops were not only trained professionally, but also had collected intelligence information on Hong Kong's defence systems, and knew where the most fatal parts were for invading Hong Kong. Japanese spies were everywhere in the city before the war. Especially those Japanese monks among the Japanese community, who carried metal bowls and would strike them while walking everywhere, then draw maps. I was glad I didn’t give them even one penny.

The battle left over five thousand soldiers killed and wounded, and seven thousand civilians killed and wounded. Also, at least ten thousand soldiers were captured, including Andrew’s comrades.

What I believed was that Hong Kong had done her best. The British, Canadians, Indians and the Chinese fiercely resisted till the end.

7.3. The Thief Tam

Since that ‘Black Christmas’, my life had changed, along with all of Hong Kong. I couldn't let them know that I was married to the British. I was afraid that someone would inform the Japanese for a small reward and put me in a British concentration camp. Everything reminded Hong Kong people that this place was no longer a British colony, but a 'Hong Kong Occupied Territory' by Japan.

We needed to learn immediately to bow ninety degrees at the waist.

The Japanese could shoot anybody at any time they wanted.

Many people disappeared for no reason.

The Allied Air Force kept bombing Hong Kong against the Japanese occupation. They even dropped incendiary bombs which caused huge fires. Many houses were burned down and many residents died or were injured. The central theatre where Andrew and I had been watching movies, and that we had been to many times, all on fire. Afterwards, people learned that using water would cause fire to burn more and more violently, only sand could do the firefighting. People started to reserve buckets of sand to stand by. As did I.

As soon as I heard the familiar sounds of the planes, I hid inside my camphor trunk and closed the lid, leaving a little gap for air. Inside were some of Andrew's old clothes and my wedding dress, along with all my valuable belongings. On the worst nights, I would think if I died, I would die with all I had.

Hong Kong was suffering from war. Except for the Japanese, all Hong Kong people were hungry. Every morning, at least a few hundred people never woke up. There was a black wooden car driving slowly along the street, collecting corpses, and dumping them into mass graves. The starving Hong Kong was a pathetic sight.

One day, I was walking to Pauline's home in Kowloon. A man flew past me, chased by another man behind.

'Snatched thing! Snatched!' he yelled loudly, hoping he could get help. The first man suddenly stopped and shoved something into his mouth. The second man rushed to him to grab it from his mouth and kicked him until he fell to the ground. The second man finally got a small piece of beef back; he was panting and cursing, 'Damn you, you snatched my beef. I bought it for my wife's confinement.'

The man who was sitting on the street with two hands covering his stomach, his eyes were closed, his mouth was still chewing, and red blood seeped from the corners of his mouth, which was the beef blood. He looked satisfied. The crowd of spectators pointed at him and cursed, although all of them, like me, were hungry. I didn't point my finger at this poor man, who had to steal.

'As long as he ate the beef. Death by being beaten, with a full stomach, is better than death from hunger,' Pauline said and sighed when I told her what I just saw.

Pauline was grilling a fish in the kitchen. 'May, look at the fatty fish, so fresh,' she said jovially, 'Tam gave it to me this morning, I don't know where he stole it from this time.'

Tam was one of those who fled to Hong Kong from the mainland before Hong Kong fell into Japanese hands. He was homeless and huddled in the stairway of Pauline's building at night, looking for food everywhere during the day.

But he was only stealing, not robbing, he told us.

'Pauline, I'll give you a piece of pork bone to eat. I found it in the market,' Tam stopped Pauline on the stairs one day. From then on, whenever Tam found any raw meat, he gave it to Pauline to cook and always asked, 'Is May coming today?'

Of course, we would leave him his portion to eat. If Tam didn't find food, he would go outside the Japanese dining hall and queue up for others to buy leftovers. Those leftovers were wiped down from the Japanese dining tables. Kind people would give Tam a bowl of food because he queued for them in the cold wind.

Most of the time, Tam like many others, was hungry day and night. That night was a croaker fish, the size of a palm. Fried until golden and fragrant by Pauline.

'Oh dear, the fish head came off,' Pauline said. 'What a pity.'

'Tam was asking about you, just before you arrived. He said he would come back for fish. Where has he gone now?' Pauline said while putting congee into my bowl. 'He looked panicky and hurried, he said he had a big deal this time.'

Tam did not come that night, and didn't come any other nights after. His place was occupied by someone else. A week later, we found out from neighbours that Tam was beaten to death on the street for stealing a char siu bun.

'No wonder the fish head came off that day, it has never happened to me before. You know I am very good at cooking fish. Well, no more fish, no more meat now, May: we must go vegetarian.' Pauline turned around and started snoring next to me in bed.

I stared at the top of the mosquito net and thought, what did Tam want to tell me? Did he go to hell or heaven as the Bible says? All I knew was that this man came to Hong Kong from Fat San, he was only twenty-four years old, the same age as Pauline, born in the Year of the Sheep, an orphan, and grew up on the streets of his hometown.

I was also very worried about my brothers in the mainland. Gok, whether he had met the Japanese yet, and Kai, whether he had rice in his bowl. I hadn't heard from them for long time.

The turmoil and torment of war was drowning everyone.

7.4. Looking For Andrew

The camps in Stanley and Sham Shui Po were set up by the Japanese for British soldiers and British officers with families. This included Lieutenant Colonel S. White, who was the commander of the 2nd Royal Scots—Andrew's regiment, the main troop force in the Battle of Hong Kong, and Major General Christopher Michael Maltby. They, along with their soldiers, were gruesomely tortured inside, and many of them died.

Sir Mark Aitchison Young, the Governor of Hong Kong was locked in The Peninsula Hotel and soon transferred to a Taiwanese prisoner camp. He suffered a lot and was even imprisoned in a bamboo cage. Then he was transferred to an allied prisoner-of-war camp in north China. People thought he would not survive, but he did.

I heard that in the prison camp in Sham Shui Po, the British soldiers were suffering from starvation to where they even ate all the mice. I decided to go to the Sham Shui Po prisoner camp and convinced Pauline to come with me one day. I bought bread and biscuits and oranges. We threw them inside over the wire and shouted as quietly as we could: 'Come here, there is something to eat!'

A man walked over slowly. I had never seen such a tall and thin foreigner. His light blonde hair grew to his shoulders, his eyes were like two big holes, and his cheeks were sunken like a hollowed-out bitter gourd. He smiled at us and bent over to pick it up, raised his hand and told us to leave quickly.

Just before walking a few steps, I suddenly heard someone singing—it was a Japanese song. A Japanese soldier with a rifle was coming from a distance and his bayonet flashed a golden light in the afterglow.

Pauline froze. Immediately, I pulled her into the bushes by the side of the road. We dared not breathe. My mind was thinking: what kind of story would I make up in case I got caught? Pauline trembled and I grasped her arms.

Finally, the Japanese singing faded away.

For the rest of the day, Pauline kept berating me for pulling her there because she nearly wet herself. That night I said to Pauline, 'If Andrew is inside, he won't come out alive. He would starve to death because he can't eat rice without throwing up.'

'I think your *gweilo* husband would eat mud. Not rice? Now? You don't even know if he is dead or still alive,' Pauline said angrily while washing her dry, cracked feet in the basin of water.

'Why don't you ask Sang to find out? He came again yesterday. He said he is going to south-east China near Singapore to join the British troops.' Pauline wiping her feet, moved the basin into the kitchen keeping the water for the next use, maybe to clean our urine bucket.

'He said he went to your home but you weren't in, as always. He thought you were here,' Pauline said. 'Sang hasn't given up on you, May, he hasn't.'

I met Sang outside my home on the street. His appearance had matured a lot, but he still had not changed his feelings of a passionate youth about his country.

On the morning of December 8th 1941, after he had just completed his two months of training, his team received a call from their boss who told them that the Japanese were bombing the airport, and they must take action immediately.

'We shot down one Japanese airplane. We were so excited to see it fall into the sea,' he told me. 'Eight of us Chinese controlled one anti-aircraft gun, and eight Indians had another one. We fought very hard.' He showed his smile, 'The senior officer rewarded us with a sheep. We cooked curry lamb which the Indian fellows could enjoy too. It was so delicious.'

Sang and his comrades held their ground position with incredible valour till they couldn't hold it anymore. Sang took advice from the Indian fellow to change uniforms and run back home. He came home without any injury, apart from exhaustion.

He said, 'May, I have decided to go to the mainland first, then from there I will go to Burma and India. I am going to help the British and Chinese troops fight against Japan. I will work as a civilian at the air base,' he said. I was very amazed by his bravery.

'I haven't heard from my husband for a long time. I don't know if he is alive or dead,' I said. 'I want you to bring him a letter for me.' I showed him a folded piece of paper and insisted he take off his coat. 'I'm going to sew this inside your coat, Sang. You will help me, won't you?' I looked into his eyes.

On that letter folded into a long strip, I wrote: 'My darling husband, long time no news from you. Hoping you are safe. I am very good and not hungry. Your darling wife, Doris.'

Andrew's first letter was also the last letter he sent from India, four weeks after he left Hong Kong.

He said: 'My darling wife… I have to eat rice if I am not to die. Curried rice is tasty. I told you I was going steal the rubies from the Indian women's foreheads—I can't now because they are not real, just painted. Not sure where we will go next. Will write to you when I possibly can. Everything seems good, no worries. Don't forget to use the money, I know you don't want to… With all my love, your husband.'

One month later, Sang returned to Hong Kong from the mainland. He told me that he couldn't find Andrew and heard that he had been killed in battle. 'I will take care of you, May, I will find a job, whatever it is. At least I will have food for you,' he added.

I didn't answer him. I wasn't sure Andrew was gone.

Soon, news confirmed that on February 15th 1942, the British forces in Singapore had surrendered to the Japanese after only eight days of battle, ten days shorter than Hong Kong's surrender. It was the largest surrender by British forces in history. Churchill would later call the surrender 'The worst disaster… in British history.' About five thousand soldiers died, eight thousand were sent to prisoner camps, and thousands more died of torture and in agony due to the inhumane treatment of the prisoners by the Japanese. Not many of them could survive till the end of the war.

'Even if Andrew is still alive, would you still have a chance to see each other again? And when?' Sang asked me.

I told him I would wait till the war ended. I needed to wait for Andrew's death to be confirmed.

Soon after, Sang joined the secret organisation which collected information to help rescue prisoners when he was helping his father's soap factory business.

The day after the Japanese occupied Hong Kong, they announced that they would replace Hong Kong's currency with the military tickets they issued. Hong Kong dollars became illegal currency and could no longer be circulated and purchased in the market. All those who had Hong Kong dollars at home were required to exchange them for military tickets, otherwise they would be subject to heavy fines.

One hundred Hong Kong dollars was equivalent to only fifty military tickets, and later only exchanged for twenty-five military tickets—the value kept shrinking. However, the Hong Kong dollar was still recognised outside Hong Kong, so Hong Kong dollar trading activity in the black market was still very active. Like Sang's father. He secretly used them to buy goods and supplies from the mainland. They didn't know where the Japanese received the information, but one day a group of armed Japanese rushed into Sang's house, searched everywhere and found them. They confiscated all the Hong Kong dollars and imposed on Sang's father very heavy fines. The only choice left for Sang's father was to sell the factory to pay the debt.

He died of a sudden illness soon after.

'My father died by Japanese hands, May. Now we are pawning my mother's jewellery for food.' Sang looked sad and angry.

Those days, Sang was like a family member to me. He insisted on hanging around and brought me some vegetables, a small bag of dried lemons, or a few rock sugars. Simply, Sang was waiting.

Knowing he was always there for me, it was like having a piece of wood I could hold onto when drowning. Andrew was always alive in my thoughts, he had never gone away. We had vows, and I believed in them.

7.5. My Landlady Mrs Wen Begs for Her Life

I was almost penniless. Andrew's deposits in Shanghai Bank could not be withdrawn, the little bank book was like waste paper. The rent had not been paid. I was starting to eat less and less, like most people. Rumours of the char siu buns stuffed with dead body meat sold in the city terrified me. One day when I returned from Pauline's home, everything in my apartment was stolen except my camphor trunk, which was at a standstill beside my bed. The solid copper bolt lock had been beaten badly but was still set. I was so glad that before leaving home I didn't forget to hide my marriage certificate inside my shoes, under the insoles, and my wedding ring, in the hidden pocket underneath my coat's lining. Since Andrew left home, the only, most safe place, was myself.

I decided to move to Kowloon, to a village called Sha Tau Kok just next to the mainland. I begged my landlord that if a letter arrived for me, to keep it for me safely and I would pay him when I came back to collect them. But I never received one.

I began my little business, buying and selling. I bought some groceries in the urban area and sold them to villagers or even would cross the border to the mainland.

My new landlord Mr Wen and his wife were Hakka speakers. They had two children. Mr Wen farmed the fields at home. Mrs

Wen was a competent woman. She was doing the same business as me. But her business was bigger and more dangerous.

Mrs Wen crossed the border to the mainland twice a week. She didn't want to go through the checkpoint, because you needed to grease the palms of border guards who could be Japanese, or Chinese who were working for the Japanese. 'The good things are taken away by the guards,' Mrs Wen said, 'That is what happened to me almost every time. I was once captured by the Japanese on my way back and made to build a road with mud for three days. Everything was confiscated.' I admired Mrs Wen's bravery, and also worried for her.

After dark, Mrs Wen was ready to go. She had two big cloth bags, one hung on her stomach and one on her back. They were always full of stuff she bought in the city she was sure would sell well, as well as any dried cabbage, pickled black olives—anything grown on their land.

Two days later, when Mrs Wen sneaked back home from the mainland, she carried the same bags full of stuff she bought from the mainland. It could be rice, biscuits, meat, or old clothes—some of them were well-made. That was the reason her children's clothes were quite nice, they were not dressed like countryside people, I thought.

Mrs Wen and some other people like her would cross a small river where there was a wire fence with empty tins hanging. If one was touched by someone then all the tins made sounds. Next would be some handheld torch lights crossing in the dark; sometimes there would be some shooting and shouting. Everyone's heart would sink in the village.

One night we heard horrible shouting. I heard Mr Wen get up and open the door. I knew his wife was on the way back home that night. I opened my eyes and waited too.

Hours and hours, almost dawn. I heard Mrs Wen come in finally.

The next day, while Mr Wen was cooking congee for his wife, he told me she was nearly killed last night. Luckily she hid underwater covered up by miscellaneous trees till the shooting stopped, the lighting went off, and when everything went quiet, she sneaked away from the water. Very soon, I saw Mrs Wen was on the road again.

One afternoon, a group of Japanese passed by, and one of them fancied a brown silk shirt which hung on the bamboo pole under the sun to dry. He was going to take it as his horse-riding lampshade. It was Mrs Wen's ten-year-old son's best shirt. Mrs Wen hurriedly stepped forward, bowed ninety degrees, and clasped her palms together again, begging the Japanese soldier not to take it.

'Sir, sir—please take this instead, look, it's also very good.' Mrs Wen tried to give the Japanese her brown shirt—also silk, but rough silk.

'*Baka!*' the Japanese opened his eyes wide and raised the butt of his rifle to Mrs Wen.

Stunned Mrs Wen turned around and ran away, and the Japanese soldiers chased after her frantically. Mrs Wen ran into the house, then ran through the corridors through the neighbours' houses, then to another house, then another, until the last.

She knelt on the ground and kept knocking her head down on the floor to beg for mercy, 'Sir, sir, I'm sorry, I'm sorry.' The Japanese fiercely beat her with the butt of his rifle and kicked her with his leather boots and yelled like a monster. Mrs Wen curled herself like a wax gourd. She had to lie in bed for three months.

It was very sad and frightening for me. I thought of leaving for the city. It seemed nowhere I felt safe.

One afternoon, I was cooking in the kitchen when Mrs Wen's eleven-year-old son suddenly rushed in. 'Sister May, Sister May, come out to the sun-drying patio quick, the Japanese are here to search for some people,' he called, out of breath.

The large patio was full of villagers lining up. The Japanese interpreter said with his high-pitched voice, 'Our Imperial Army received information that some people have colluded with the East River Column (an anti-Japanese guerrilla force that my brother Gok was a member of). Who are they?'

No one answered. The two Japanese started knocking down the front row with their rifle butts starting from each side.

Someone started calling out names; it was the village head. He said two names, one of which was similar to Mr Wen's name. I saw Mrs Wen, who was still very weak, almost faint. I held Mrs Wen's daughter's hand tightly, the nine-year-old girl was shaking involuntarily. Afterwards, she told me that one of the fiercest Japanese had given her some sweets before.

Those two men were tied with ropes and dragged behind the horses the Japanese soldiers were riding on. The Japanese were riding slowly then suddenly whipped the horses amid their wild laughter. I saw these two men stumble and dragged to the ground like two bundles of firewood. Their cries were ghastly. They were inundated with water, then made to vomit by pressing their stomachs with a bamboo pole, and tortured at the Japanese camp all night. Three days later, they were carried home by their families.

They had nothing to do with the East River Column, they were both just honest farmers. The village head became the most hated person.

'What could he do? Otherwise, more people would suffer or even be shot dead, don't you think May?' Mrs Wen said with a long sigh.

Soon after, one day the pale-faced Mrs Wen came to my room and said, 'May, you better move out of the village back to the urban area. I heard that girls from other villages were taken into Japanese military camps, and they were released after several days and nights. Those girls…' Tears dropped from Mrs Wen's eyes.

The next day, I went back to Hong Kong Island. Only a few months later, I heard that Mrs Wen died of pain. She was only thirty-three.

7.6. Mr Kuroda's Swift Beatings

I was staying with Pauline and was doing my old business—selling well-prepared fruit in the clubs. The people who came to the club the most were the Japanese and the Chinese who had jobs with the Japanese. 'Don't go to those kind of places, you might get raped by those bad men. A lot of Japanese in those clubs,' Sang tried to stop me. 'I will take care of you, May, don't go,' he begged.

He did go into business. He bought fresh green beans and cooked them with salt, put them in a big glass tin, slung them over his shoulders, and sold them along the street near the theatre. I once saw him from a distance: he couldn't sell much, only sweated a lot on his back. The wealthy boy was long gone.

One day, I picked up the Hong Kong daily newspaper left by the guests and read it. A Japanese officer raised his hand and called me over. He asked me in Cantonese: 'You know how to read?'

'…Not much, I learned old books when I was a child,' I answered apprehensively.

'Read this to me, could you?' He smiled, and casually pointed to the front page of the newspaper.

'The Japanese Army and Air Force attacked Hengyang. The fierce air battle resulted in a decisive battle between Japan and the United States. The Japanese army on the Leizhou Peninsula attacked Shicheng.'

'Good, very good,' he looked very satisfied, 'I'll write a note for you, take it with you to our airport team. You will get a job.'

In the evening two days later, I was outside the office of the Chu Cheng Group at the Kai Tak Airport construction site.

I had arranged to share a room with another Chinese girl, a teacher, who introduced herself as Miss Lo. Her father was a famous architect in Hong Kong at that time. She also was the daughter-in-law of a matched wealthy family.

Three years into her marriage, she showed no signs of pregnancy. She drank a lot of Chinese medicine as advised by her mother and her mother-in-law.

'Although they were of terrible taste, I didn't mind drinking them all every night,' she told me.

After days and days, her husband's family had lost their patience, and so did her husband who was the only son. A concubine had to be welcomed to the house. Within a year, the concubine gave birth to twins, a boy and a girl. The Chinese call that 'Dragon and Phoenix'. The house was full of joy, except for Miss Lo.

Of course, following that, she had lost out of love from her husband, and favour with her husband's family; she was often suffering from her mother-in-law's scorn. 'My mother-in-law said "Even raised chickens will lay eggs, I don't know if it's because your belly is full of poetry and books,"' Miss Lo smiled wryly.

She lost her job as a teacher after the Japanese took over, but was recommended to the Chu Cheng Group. She moved out from home.

'No one asked me to stay, even my husband. It was so hard to believe that he said I was his only woman, his only love. We had known each other since childhood.' I could hear Miss Lo's voice choking up.

'All of my family members have gone to the United States. I want to stay in Hong Kong. If I marry someone, I will always belong to my husband.' Miss Lo was saddened. 'As my mother said: Marry a chicken then you must follow that chicken; marry a dog, then you must follow that dog.'

I believed she was still in love with her husband and was waiting for him to come and take her home one day. But I never saw a man come to visit her when I lived with her for a year and a half.

The Chu Cheng Group used many allied prisoners of war as labourers to build two more concrete runways; some of them were Chinese workers. Every day, the workers put stones dug out of the cave into a single-wheeled wooden truck, then they and the trucks would descend the mountain fast, along the single track coming down, which was very dangerous. A little out of mind, and you and the truck would run off the track. Injury, even death, happened often.

My job with Miss Lo was to register their shipments. When I looked up at those workers running down, I was always on edge.

The manager of the Chu Cheng Group was named Kuroda. Originally, he was the owner of a silk shop on Nathan Road, and he nodded and bowed to customers all day long. He suddenly changed his kimono into a military uniform when the Japanese landed in Hong Kong. His humble, smiling face instead now was bordering on arrogance.

'My mother and I used to go to his shop to buy silk for dresses. Luckily he seems not to recognise me,' Miss Lo told me. 'He was so humble—look at him now.'

Kuroda liked to stand beside the tracks, staring at each rickety wooden truck going down to see who wasn't fast enough and whose cart wasn't full enough. I only saw the workers fall to the ground and groan in anguish, but did not see Kuroda beating them.

'His beatings are invisible, ruthless and fast, without you even noticing,' Miss Lo whispered to me.

Since I worked in the Chu Cheng Group, I had a place to live and meals to eat and I was also sent to school to learn Japanese.

Apart from Pauline and Sang, I never told anyone about my days working for the Japanese and that I could speak and write a little bit. Pauline was quite happy when I brought food to her. Sang said, 'You must be careful, May, I wish you didn't have to work for the Japanese.'

I also didn't tell Miss Lo that my husband was a British soldier. I told her I was still single. She once asked me, 'May, why do you want to learn English with me so much?'

'I hope to marry a *gweilo* one day and go far, far away,' I replied jokingly. She taught me a lot of English.

In August 1945, the Japanese surrendered after they occupied Hong Kong for three years and eight months. I heard that Miss Lo went back to teaching at school. She didn't eventually go back to her husband's home, and never got married again.

8. On My Way to England

April, 1946. With a deep whistle, the *Small Striker* ship carrying hundreds of people moved offshore slowly from the Victoria Harbour of Hong Kong.

It started a more than four-week voyage. I was on that ship, among other Chinese wives of British soldiers. Some of them had children, like Connie, who had six-year-old and four-year-old sons, and Susan, whose daughter was five years old. Jenny and I were on our own. We all had almost identical camphor trunks. Both Connie and Susan even had two of them. My one was the largest and the most beautiful.

When the porters carried my dark brown camphor trunk walking across the ship's deck, I looked up. The copper decor was so shiny. My most important belongings I had folded very carefully and tidied into ordered piles. At the bottom was my wedding dress; inside of it, my marriage certificate, which was well plastered on letter paper; then Andrew's cashmere cardigan—a gift I bought—and above that, Andrew's letters. I knew that when I lifted the lid, the scent of camphor wood would be so fresh, all over the place. Everything inside was going to be as it was.

8.1 Andrew Was Alive

On August 30th 1945, British Rear Admiral Sir Cecil Halliday Jepson Harcourt sailed into Hong Kong on the HMS *Swiftsure* to re-establish the British Government's control over the colony. He formally accepted the Japanese surrender on September 16th. Hong Kong was finally back under the British flag again.

Kuroda came to our accommodation. He stood outside and said he must thank me and Miss Lo for our hard work. He was going home. He looked sad and in a state of utter dejection.

I left Chu Cheng Group the next day.

On a sunny morning, I went to the British Army headquarters in the Guangdong Provincial Bank. I was there looking for any information about my husband Andrew.

I hoped for some unexpected news, that he was alive, but was starved to a skeleton, like the man I saw in the Sham Shui Po Prisoner Camp. It would be easy to put more pounds on him just with my char siu pork as soon as he came back to me. Or maybe he had lost one leg, in the hospital, and was waiting to be sent home but had been told that his wife wasn't living at that address anymore, that no one else knew where she had gone, and then I would find him crying in the ward.

I walked into the Major's office and showed him my marriage certificate and wedding photo. He looked at me with a bit of surprise and said, 'I've seen your picture in a church in India. I've seen Andrew Devlin praying with a picture of his wife. He told me that he lost his wife during an Allied plane bombing.'

'Thank God,' the Major said with a smile. 'Your husband went back to Edinburgh in early 1942 because he had gastric disease. Must have been very bad.'

I smiled wryly. 'My husband and I both seem to have been resurrected from the dead.'

Walking out of the building of the Guangdong Provincial Bank, I stood on the steps and looked at the soldiers passing by, I felt myself very short. I didn't know if I wanted to laugh or cry.

'Doris, Doris, darling,' a tall, thin man came up to me in a trot. I couldn't believe he was Dr Selwyn-Clarke. He gave me a big hug. He was so happy to see me as well. When I told him my husband was found alive, he was thrilled and held my hands dancing in the corridor. My tears started to run down my cheeks.

Dr Selwyn-Clarke was the head of the colony's Medical Department before the Japanese ruled Hong Kong. He looked so skinny. Almost like he was only skin hanging on his bones.

I could not forget that day, just at the beginning of the Japanese occupation, I found Pauline lying on her bed, grey-faced, bathed in perspiration.

'I am going to die? I'm going to die, May, save me, save me,' she groaned in agony. I was in huge shock seeing her, whom I called my older sister, dying. My only thought was getting her to the hospital. I ran to the hospital nearby. I was told they only accepted patients who were in military families. I took off my right shoe and pulled out the black insole. There, was an oblong-shaped piece of paper—the certificate of my marriage. It had been shredded into pieces. I showed him a small cut photo of me and Andrew that I hid in the waistband of my trousers.

'I am a British wife, she is my sister,' I said impatiently, opening those pieces with great care. The Chinese man who was the matron of the hospital turned to an ambulance that had just arrived. A Western man was getting out of the driver's seat. Beard stubble and red eyes could not hide his spirit—Dr Clarke. I just knew he was going to help me.

Pauline was carried down to Dr Clarke's ambulance by stretcher from the second floor. The doctor told me that if I had been half an hour late, Pauline would have died.

Dr Clarke also gave me a small bag of rice which was at an extreme shortage. Since then, I had seen Dr Clarke sometimes as he continued to work around the hospitals and the Informal Welfare Committee during the beginning of the Japanese occupation of Hong Kong. Until he was arrested by the Japanese, and given a death sentence. He was locked into a very small cell under the Hong Kong Supreme Court and then sent to the Stanley Internment Camp with his wife and their six-year-old daughter.

It was he who organised all the British military families to live together in a few different places, who concentrated support and helped their lives while waiting to be shipped back to England.

8.2. The Women I Lived with in the Villa

Dr Clarke arranged for me to live with Susan, Jenny and Connie in a villa. We were Chinese wives waiting to be sent to England, our husbands' home, all of whom had all been informed.

That beautiful two-floored villa had a garden and roof terrace; it had been the home of a highly-ranked Japanese military officer during their occupation of Hong Kong. Now it was one of the British families' temporary accommodations.

At the front of the garden on the right, there was a tall white champaca gardenia flower tree. In springtime, flowers frilled, blooming like snow-white jade, as faint fragrance delicate and sweet, wafted secluded across the street. A bauhinia tree bloomed with purple flowers on the left side. Those flowers became the emblem of Hong Kong. The cicadas perched on branches at night would chant, like lullabies.

I always lay on my bed, often unable to get to sleep; my eyes would stay open until the first rays of the morning sun. I thought over and over again—was I making the right decision to leave everything behind for a country I didn't know, to a man, who I had thought was dead and I hadn't seen for four and a half years? So had he. And his love still stood like his letters said? In my camphor trunk were those letters Andrew wrote to me since he found out I was alive. Every letter was a plea: 'Come to England. I miss you, my darling wife.' Always.

I wrote to my brothers and told them my decision that I was going to England to be with Andrew, and would come back if things didn't turn out as I expected—I had my money ready to do so.

Gok wrote me back with a photo of him and Kai. They looked handsome and happy. Gok's letter was ten-pages long. Mostly it was how much they didn't want me to go to a strange country on my own.

I found out that Gok had left the National Army to join the East River Column three years before. Established by the Guangdong People's anti-Japanese guerrilla force, they rescued prisoners like British soldiers and important Chinese and American pilots; protected traders in Kowloon and Guangzhou; attacked the police station at Tai Po, and bombed Kai Tak Airport. They also killed Chinese traitors and those who collaborated with the Japanese. They did anything they could do to wreck the Japanese rule in Hong Kong.

I guess he thought that what he was doing meant he was protecting his sister in Hong Kong. I didn't know what he had done.

Years later, I was so glad he did that because the East River Column guerrillas were later recognised by Mao's Communist Party. It protected him from the cruel torment in later China.

The hardest thing was telling Sang. We met at a small garden not far from the villa.

'May, if he lied, if he doesn't love you any more, if he has had another woman, he may be asking you to come just to make himself look good, nothing else,' Sang said anxiously when I told him my decision.

'I swore an oath before God; I must not fail to keep my word,' I said. 'Find a girl to marry, don't come back to me again,' I begged.

He cried sitting on the grass.

I couldn't forget his calling out behind me: 'May… May…'

Tears flowed down my face all the way back to the villa. That goodbye was as long as our lifetimes.

Susan—the Marine's Wife

The first day I met Susan, she was sitting on the sofa quietly while Connie and Jenny were chatting to each other. She gave me a smile when she saw me walk in, moved her seat, and beckoned me to sit next to her. A little girl was sitting on a large brown camphor trunk which was quite similar to my own. She was Susan's daughter, Lily—she looked more Western, had a high nose bridge, pale skin and big eyes, but was a very shy girl; she fluttered her long eyelashes when biting her nails. She was a quiet one like her mother.

Susan was the only daughter of a corner shop owner in Wan Chai. A tall and thin British marine kept coming back to buy cigarettes, or anything else, after the first time he saw her. Soon they married and lived above the shop.

Her father had warned her before she decided to marry a foreigner: 'Don't blame me that I didn't tell you that if you marry a chicken then you follow the chicken; if you marry a dog then you have to follow the dog. Now you insist on marrying a *gweilo:* you will be his woman forever, you must follow him. There is no return.'

When Susan's husband was sent to India, Susan didn't even know she was pregnant with Lily. I could see that little Lily was much more excited than her mother about going to England.

Connie—the Navy Engineer's Wife

Two boys chased each other and ran around between the camphor trunks and other furniture in the living room, pretending to fly airplanes. They were Connie's six and four-year-old sons.

Connie was lame in her right leg because she had polio when was she three years old. Her wealthy parents did everything to give their daughter the best.

'If I wasn't lame, I wouldn't have married a Western soldier,' she said once.

Connie was well educated. She studied in a private school, in a continental European-style big house halfway up the Hong Kong Peak. The teachers were those from mainland China who had escaped the turbulence, and those from English or American religious circles. Thus Connie spoke fluent English.

When she was only nineteen, Connie's parents opened an English learning school for her in Causeway Bay. Her husband was hired as a part-time teacher. He was a Navy engineer. Connie liked him a lot. He was from London, a quiet young man.

Connie's mother started to invite him to their home for dinner. Their large family house was very eye-catching in Sheung Wan. Then they started to date and married after Connie got pregnant.

They lived happily in a three-bedroom apartment on the next road—a wedding gift from Connie's parents.

When Connie's husband was shipped to India at the same time as Andrew, their son was nearly two. She only found out she was pregnant with their second child two months after her husband left.

'The pregnancy was hellish,' Connie said, 'even only a tiny drop of cooking oil on top of the steamed eggs would make me vomit.'

Connie's younger son had never met his father, like Lily.

At our dinner table one night Connie told us that her beautiful family home was bombed by the Japanese. Her parents and her two brothers along with most of the household did not survive. Luckily her own home was not bombed. But the windows had been smashed down. If she'd had no son, who was crying in her arms, she would have killed herself to be with them together.

She said her father insisted on not going to the shelter. 'My father always said that the Japanese are just "white turnip heads"—he was never going to be scared by the Japanese. Look, what consequences. He left me alone in this world.'

Jenny—the RAF Kai Tak Officer's Wife

Jenny was so proud and so looking forward to seeing her husband from the first day in the villa. She couldn't wait to show us his photos, a very handsome and charming officer in a smart uniform. We sometimes laughed at her because she was always holding her husband's photo and talking to him under the duvet before sleeping.

When pretty Jenny met her husband she was studying in a well-known girl's school. At that time, Jenny was just like a lot of other young people who were prepared to sacrifice themselves to save their country. She was a good singer who performed in the street to demonstrate against the devilish Japanese killings in mainland China like me and Sang. Her enthusiastic heart was melted by RAF officer, Johnathan.

'Jenny and Johnny,' he said. She believed they had the same enemies and the same ambitions. He proposed to her before he was sent to Southeast Asia. Jenny gave him a lot of handkerchiefs embroidered with 'JJ'.

'I used seven different colours of silk thread. Johnny can use different colours on different days,' she told me.

Before the Japanese invasion of Hong Kong, Jenny's parents were journalists. During the time of Japanese rule in Hong Kong, they were members of the British Army Aid Group. Those people would risk their lives to rescue prisoners. Jenny was one of those brave people.

'I was almost captured by the Japanese when I delivered the leaflets,' Jenny once said, 'but I hid them under my belly pretending I was pregnant. The Japanese even asked whether I needed help. I said "*eyi eyi*" (no no).' I still remember her lovely cunning smile and her dimples when she told us that.

'You could have ended up in jail, Jenny,' I said. I couldn't imagine what would have happened to her if she'd been caught.

'I am the smartest girl in the world, my father always said that,' Jenny laughed.

Mrs Forende—the Jewish Painter

Mrs Forende was the last person to join our group; the Chinese wives of British soldiers.

One day when Norman, a young soldier, charged his jeep up the hill and stopped outside our villa, I saw a middle-aged woman seated in the front and a mountain of boxes in the back seat. I knew she must be Mrs Forende whom Dr Clarke told me would come to stay with us.

'Doris, if you don't mind, she is going to share your room. She has just come from Shanghai, she is a painter,' he told me.

I thought there must have been no more room for her where the European families stayed, the Four Seasons Hotel, about a fifteen minute walk from us.

'The *gweipo* (female foreigner) is coming,' I told the wives. They all rushed to the living room window, including the kids.

I opened the door, and like a gust of wind, she hugged me, almost wrapping me completely in her chest. The smell of sweat and perfume filled my nose powerfully at the same time. Later she told me the perfume was No. 5. It was easy to remember the name. I didn't know that it was also an expensive perfume. I had to wait years to buy my first bottle.

'You must be the little darling, Doris.' Her voice was so loud, full of happiness. It seemed like I was her old friend who she was so desperate to see again.

'Oh, you are a pretty little one. Just as Dr Clarke told me.' She pushed away a bit to look at me from top to bottom. I was glad that I did some preparation for my hair and dress. I liked her and liked her a lot. She was a bright, hearty and candid Western woman, I thought.

'Nice room Doris, I love it,' Mrs Forende said walking into my room on the first floor. She stood standing by the window looking outside. 'What a beautiful view Doris. We must be friends because we are going to be living together for a few months.' She turned to me and winked while taking off her hat—she had short black hair like me.

Once Mrs Forende moved in, there always was a light silvery laugh ringing out from the living room when she was with us.

She ate what we ate. And surprisingly, she could make very good Shanghai Bao.

'I lived a very long time in Shanghai,' she explained.

She taught us English and how to eat like decent English people.

'Darling Doris,' she said, 'you must butter your toast slowly, like this,' Mrs Forende smiled. 'Then, cut it into small pieces, open your mouth, put it in, and keep your lipstick in place.'

'Don't put your teaspoon into your mouth to drink your tea, Susan,' she shouted with laughter.

'Oh, no, Jenny, hasn't your husband told you how to have your soup? Tilt the bowl slightly outwards and spoon the last of the soup, don't pour the bowl with the soup up to your mouth.'

'Oh my God, Connie, who told you to use your left hand to hold the fork?' she opened her eyes wide exaggeratedly.

'I am left-handed, Mrs Forende,' Connie replied hastily.

'Oh, I am sorry, but can you try not to do so?' Mrs Forende insisted. Poor Connie did try. But one day, Mrs Forende said to her, 'Darling Connie, just use your left hand—looking at you eat, it is too painful.'

She told us that if your mother-in-law opened her arms to you when you walked into her house the first time, it meant she liked you and you were going to have good days in England.

She taught us how to write letters, then pretended to be each of us, and read them. Then she wrote a reply, pretending to be the husband, and read it gruffly. This became the most lively show of the week. I was the wife who received more letters than others.

'It's here again, here again, Doris, your letter. How could you not tell us what your Andrew has written?' Mrs Forende would always shake her head exaggeratedly to make fun of me.

Between my bed and Mrs Forende's bed was only a small western-style dressing table under the window, it was a shining brown colour with golden decorations. On the table were mostly Mrs Forende's things. There was always a bottle of red wine.

She started to drink after washing—we all used a metal bucket, mixing boiled water and cold water, using a small towel to soak the warm water to clean ourselves. We talked when she was drinking. When the wine was finished to the last drop, most of the time, Mrs Forende fell asleep. Through the mosquito net, I could still see Mrs Forende toss around every night in bed. She seemed to never actually sleep. Sometimes, she sat up suddenly with a confused look.

I didn't know what she had been through in mainland China. I pretended I was sleeping. The next day, she was back to the daytime Mrs Forende: happy and loud.

Mrs Forende's husband was a British Jew. She met him when she came to London from Germany as a twenty-five-year-old young girl in 1924.

'He is a writer for theatre—romantic and passionate, like a crazy person,' Mrs Forende kept telling me though she knew I may not understand fully. 'We quarrelled all the time,' she said dreamily. 'Once he threw a lipstick at me. It hit my forehead forcefully; I was bleeding.' She reached out of the mosquito net, opened the wine bottle, and poured more wine into her half-full glass—that wasn't what she normally did.

'I left London for Germany the next day. He was begging me at the station, crying. But I was furious. I kept hitting his hands when he was holding onto the window.' She took a slug of the wine.

'Since then, we haven't seen each other for seven years—three years longer than you, Doris.' She smiled ruefully at me.

Mrs Forende was given a visa to come to China by Mr Ho, who was the Chinese ambassador in Vienna when all countries had closed their doors to the Jewish people. It was December 1938.

'At the time, I was still angry at him. And I also didn't believe they wanted to kill us. My father was a doctor,' Mrs Forende said. Her parents insisted on staying in Germany, they didn't want to leave their home.

'You go, for us, they said.' Mrs Forende upended the glass and swallowed it all.

'They died soon after being sent to the camp. I knew they were not going to survive.' Mrs Forende was holding back her tears with her broken voice.

She was at sea for two months, along with thousands of Jewish people. She got very badly seasick and couldn't get up. It was a painful voyage. 'When the ship finally arrived in Shanghai, I was almost the first to squeeze out of the ship, but I didn't know where to go—no one does I thought.' Mrs Forende was falsely jovial with her mirthless laugh, 'I didn't know anyone.'

She slowly walked out of the Jewish ghetto in Shanghai and entered and exited the Shanghai Concession as a painter. She said she liked socialising with the Japanese the most and sold them her paintings.

'Whatever I said, they were more than happy to pay,' she laughed.

Her husband in London was begging her to go back to England in every letter. 'The war was raging, and I was afraid that the ship would be attacked and sunk, and planes would be shot down,' Mrs Forende explained. 'Finally, the Japanese surrounded. Here I am.'

Mrs Forende had nine boxes of her paintings stacked up in the corner of our room. She said they were all her children. She had an exhibition on Garden Avenue on Hong Kong Island while living in the villa. Her painting that sold for the highest price was for thousands of Hong Kong dollars.

'This is for you, Doris. I painted it when I was in Shanghai,' Mrs Forende held it up to show me the night before we embarked on the ship *Small Striker*. 'Doesn't it look like your father playing the erhu?' she asked. I burst into tears.

In this small painting, a blind old Chinese man was playing the erhu on the street. The sound seemed to pour out of his hands which seemed to be shaking, his dazed face looked up at the sky; his eyes, covered in a grey curtain, couldn't see any sorrow but in his music.

That day, when I went out with Mrs Forende for the last shop, we saw a blind man sitting on a small wooden stool playing the erhu on the busy Nathan Road. Beside him, a little girl was sitting on the floor looking after the chipped bowl in front of them. Sorrowfully melodic and tuneful, *Butterfly Lovers* echoed in the street. I felt as though I was seeing my father playing the erhu to express his dissatisfaction with the pain of losing his wife.

'My father played the erhu, and he could play very well,' I stopped and told Mrs Forende.

'Where is your father now?'

'He died. Not long after my mother passed away. My father sat on a bamboo chair, facing the open door, and just played and played. I thought he was talking to my mother.' I held my tears and told her. Mrs Forende put her arm around my shoulder and drew me close to her, gently tapping a few times.

8.3. My First Voyage

The *Small Striker* had been at sea for twenty-eight days. Across the Indian Ocean, around Cape Town—now we were in the Atlantic Ocean.

The big storm last night had turned many people upside down. Mrs Forende thought she was going to die. She took off her purse from her waist and shoved it into my arms, 'Doris, it is yours, I'm dying, my God! This ship isn't sailing, it's just spinning.'

I wiped up her vomit with a towel, sat on her bed and comforted her, 'After this stop, the next stop will be fine.'

'Darling, you're also confused—you think this is a bus ride?' she groaned.

'Trust me, Mrs Forende,' I said, 'it will be almost like a bus, driving through here, there will be no wind and waves.'

'Look, I told you not to take a plane, but to take a ship with me. I thought I had experience in a big boat and could take care of you,' she gasped not wanting to vomit any more. 'Now, instead, you must look after me, I am terribly sorry, my little darling.'

The ship hit the top of the wave and then fell into the sea. It carried on all night long. The gust of wind whipped up the salty water and smashed it on our first-class balcony, howling in terror. I was quite sure that, whatever was in Mrs Forende's stomach before, was now all out. I swayed my body following the ship and held Mrs Forende with both hands. I wasn't dizzy, I wasn't vomiting and I wasn't afraid. I only just then realised that a big ship could cause such seasickness which the elegant and witty Mrs Forende was now suffering; her face now so pale and incoherent, her hair in a mess, and her champagne-coloured satin pyjamas stained with last night's food. Our dinner last night was potato soup and prime bone-in rib eye steak—my first time.

Mrs Forende was the most popular person on the whole voyage. At the first introduction dinner, the charming and outgoing Mrs Forende engaged the captain chatting for at least a half hour. The next day we had been moved to deck seven, into a large room with a balcony. The captain and crew were just above us. When we were sitting on the balcony, we could see them working with the smart uniforms on, we could even hear and wave to them. We were served at the same table by the large window. It was the one of best tables in the restaurant.

Every time, Mrs Forende would pick up the menu and read it out. She would say, 'Good choice of menu tonight, Doris, mushroom soup—that is a nice tasting soup—then cod fish with mint sauce and asparagus; or chicken fillet with Chinese vegetables.' She looked at me with a smile over the table, 'Darling, fish or chicken? Or we can order one of each to share? What do you think?'

Kind Mrs Forende knew how much English I could read. She wanted to make sure I wouldn't be embarrassed in front of the smart waiter.

Sometimes the smart Captain in his white pristine uniform came to join us. He chatted with Mrs Forende while drinking a glass of white wine, laughing loudly, drawing all the attention. Art was the topic they talked most about.

'He bought one of my paintings for thirty pounds—a good price for him,' Mrs Forende told me once, winking her eye.

8.4. A Shilling Shining in My Palm

As I had said, the *Small Striker* went on to the final stop like buses did. The storm the night before was gone in exchange for a sunny morning. The ship would soon be on shore in England that afternoon.

I looked in the mirror, my hair was done scrupulously with every detail—perfect length, just sitting at the neck, a wavy black silk. A black dress with a white collar, and a golden buckled alligator black belt sitting right on my small waistline made my breasts look firmer and bigger. I smiled.

Once, Pauline insisted on putting a wonton noodle soup bowl on my breasts. 'Wow, just the right size,' she laughed. 'People say big breasts, small brain—May, you aren't that at all.'

I made that dress for the day that I would walk down the ship and Andrew would be waiting shoreside. He would look up, smiling, with his blue eyes twinkling.

Mrs Forende came out from the bathroom. 'Oh darling, you look stunning,' she said. 'What a night, last night. Oh darling you are my brain. We did pass that bus stop,' she laughed.

'You think I should wear a scarf too? Which one do you think?' I asked.

'This one.' She picked up the black scarf with red roses and placed it around my shoulders. She gave me a big smile, 'I bet Andrew will go crazy about you, Doris.'

'You know what, Doris, I hope you will find your happiness in this country. This is a good country. It has a handsome king, who has one only wife,' she said earnestly.

Someone knocked on the door. It was Norman.

Mrs Forende waved her hand, winking at me, 'Go, go, Doris, We still have hours before the ship anchors alongside the shore.'

The deck steward in uniform approached, they were the soldiers returning home. In the warm sunshine, everybody looked happy.

Norman found a seat near the corner. He said, 'Doris, I will teach you how to use money. Look, this is one shilling, in the grocers—the same kind of shops that sell most of those things like in those in Hong Kong—you can buy some tea, bread, a packet of pudding, a bar of soap.'

'Do they sell rice?' I asked.

'I don't think they sell rice, Doris,' Norman looked disappointed, 'but I maybe can find some for you in Wales.'

'I have some rice with me,' I laughed.

'Look this is a shilling… I am going to let you have all of this money. Not much, but enough for a few days for you to buy food and stay somewhere if something goes wrong. But this one, promise me, Doris—,' he grabbed my hand, and put it on my palm. The silver lion shined under the sun.

'Don't use it on anything else, only use it to telephone me. I will come to get you. Do you understand?' He looked at me full of worry and hope. My English was enough to understand fully what he was talking about. He gave me a piece of paper. 'This is the telephone number where you can find me. Here, look.'

'There you are.' Mrs Forende walked up to the deck. She was wearing a long light-brown dress and a white jumper around her neck and shoulders. Her hair was up, fixed with an ivory-made prong. I noticed her hair stick had a carving of a happy bird with Chinese words. Similar to my mother's favourite one bought by my father. Her red nails nipped a cigarette. She took a drag and held it for a bit, the long smoke drawing out from her mouth, circling, and disappearing in the wind. She looked very relaxed and stunning. I wished that when I was forty I would be like her. I believe I have been smoking for forty years because that image of Mrs Forende smoking was always there.

Mrs Forende told us that her husband won't be waiting for her at the port because he has gone to Israel. She said, 'Do you know Doris? If your feet are not on your land, then you never can settle. I don't blame him.'

'Do you want me to help you carry your luggage, Mrs Forende?' Norman offered.

'The captain will give me a lift, he insisted last night. Oh, Norman you are such a kind young man. Don't forget to write to me and tell me if you find a girl to marry.'

Mrs Forende sat down on Norman's chair. 'Darling, he is very in love with you,' she said as he walked away. 'What a pity it is. Doris. Do you know that he quit his engineering job in Hong Kong, just for you? He wants to come back to England to be with you, what a man.'

Norman came from Wales. He was a mechanical engineer who worked for the British troops in Burma. He always drove a jeep around with his friend George between the British family camps.

One day, they stopped the jeep in front of me and Mrs Forende. With a big smile on his good-looking face, he asked, 'Where are you going ladies? Do you want a lift?' His skin was very tan and his teeth were very white.

'Yes, we want a lift,' Mrs Forende replied. She grabbed my hand jumping into the backseat.

Sometimes, when I came back to the villa after being out, I would find Norman and George sitting on the front garden balustrade. Norman jumped in front of me and said, 'Doris, why don't you want to learn how to drive? It's free, why not? Come on, Doris.' I smiled, shaking my head until the door closed behind me.

Mrs Forende said, 'This poor young man is falling for you, Doris. I have already told him that you have a husband waiting for you in Edinburgh.'

'He is just a silly boy,' I said.

'He is offering driving lessons to us, I am sure that he just wants to see you more.'

The first of Norman's driving lessons was Mrs Forende's, who got into his jeep. The jeep's noisy engine started outside on the road, bouncing down the hill with her screaming excitedly. We all laughed. I was thinking I could do better, it was only driving a car.

One evening, I was finally sitting in the driving seat after everyone else had.

'It is very easy, Doris, look,' Norman was delighted. 'This handle up; your right foot, relax a bit; hold tight this big wheel; keep both your eyes on the road, then go.' The jeep started to move before Norman finished his words.

'I have learned a lot from the girls at the dining table you know,' I said, keeping my eyes on the road.

I was also told that Norman's right shoulder had horrible scars. Mrs Forende told us he was burned in Burma. I didn't see his scars because he never took off his shirt when he was with me, no matter how hot he was.

The worst part of those driving lessons was when the jeep ploughed into someone's abandoned house's front garden and flattened a tree. Norman jumped into the driver seat and reversed the jeep in a rough grumbling sound. He shouted at me while I was standing aside in shock, 'Get in, Doris, get in, quick!'

'Damn, are you blind?' A man who looked like a servant chased after the jeep, picked up a stone and threw it at us.

That was how I learned to drive a car—with lots of laughter. The outcome of Norman's driving lessons was that it took me seven tests to get my driving licence in Edinburgh in the sixties. Sometimes I thought it must be all wrong, what I learned from him.

It was just days before we boarded the ship. Everyone in the house was busy packing. Everyone's biggest worry was not getting enough of what they could eat in England—especially the Hong Kong traditional side dishes: salted fish, dried scallops, dried cabbage, and so on. I was afraid of eating bread every day, so Guilin rice noodles and white rice were also must-haves in my suitcase. I brought many tins of dace fillets with salty black beans and luncheon meat, which Andrew liked to eat. A bag of white rice was also hidden with dried chilli and ginger, so my luggage didn't look much bigger, but was certainly the heaviest.

Norman showed up outside one afternoon. He invited me to go for a ride on that chilly evening.

'Doris, why not? Go. You are going to be at sea for weeks,' Mrs Forende shouted from the kitchen.

'Let's go to the Peak,' Norman smiled gently, a bit unlike how he usually would. The Victoria Peak had been exclusively set aside as a European residential area. No Chinese were permitted to buy or rent. The Chinese who were allowed to access were only those who worked as servants for the Europeans. The first Chinese permitted to live there was Sir

Robert Ho Tung, whose grandnephew I believe I met when I was little in our flour and rice shop. He was half-Portuguese—much more *gweilo* looking than Chinese.

We stopped at the Peak tram station. It was just back in service on Christmas Day, December 25th 1945, after the engine room was badly damaged in the attack by the Japanese.

We sat in second-class which was for the British military and the Hong Kong police force personnel. No one tried to stop me, though I should have sat in third-class with the animals. They probably thought I was Norman's wife, because he had one hand around my waist very gently when we bought the tickets. They were thirty cents.

'I am going to sit in first class, the first front seats,' Norman said like a mischievous boy. Those two seats had to be reserved for the Governor of Hong Kong. They were not available to ordinary passengers until two minutes before departure. 'It is like a London bus, this colour and those chairs,' Norman said.

That evening was a glorious sunset. Everything had been put into beautiful golden-yellow clothes. The views over the harbour and the skyscrapers of Hong Kong were still amazing in those days. Only much smaller, and the sea was at a much greater distance.

'I am going back to England with you, same ship, lower deck,' Norman said.

'Mrs Forende told us that you are working for the shipping company, earning good money. You should stay,' I said with worry.

'I will find a good job in England. Will earn as much as I do in Hong Kong. Trust me, Doris.' Norman smiled, 'I may find a job in Edinburgh.'

I shook my head lightly. Norman didn't say anything.

The afterglow of the setting sun was all swallowed up by the sea, and the rest was the cool breeze, and the shadows were mottled.

I did see him almost every day on the open deck of the ship.

8.5. A Skinny Man Walking Toward Me

The *Small Striker* dropped its anchor at the Southampton Port in the late afternoon. Slowly the ship moored. It was two days late.

The passengers started to disembark. There were a lot of laughs, tears and screaming. We were told to wait together near the exit. We were the quiet and nervous group.

I saw a tall skinny man walking toward me. He was wearing an oversized grey suit and a tie. I only recognised him by the shy smile on his clean face: that was my husband, Andrew.

'Doris,' he said, his eyes shiny.

I was trying to smile, and actually, hundreds of all sorts of feelings came up to my chest; but mostly, I just wanted to cry. We were standing face to face but didn't know what was right to do.

'You must be Andrew,' said Mrs Forende, stepping forward from behind me and giving Andrew a big hug. 'Let me tell you that your wife is my brain—Oh, you will never know how lucky you are.' Her hearty laughter suddenly made us smile a lot more naturally. 'I am going write to you, tell you all about the Doris I knew, Andrew,' she said, walking back to the captain's keep, turning her head back.

Not far from the jeep, I found Norman standing there, looking over at us quietly.

Andrew was the only husband who came to Southampton to collect his wife. He had been waiting for three days. All of the other Chinese wives were taken to London somewhere, waiting to be sent home.

'My husband told me in the letter he would be here… I don't know what is going on.' Tears burst out of Jenny's eyes, running down her face. She tried to wipe them using her handkerchief with meticulous care for her well-done makeup.

'My husband said it's too far away from Liverpool,' Susan said.

'My husband said the same. That is fine—we are going home,' Connie tried to smile and pacify her dispirited older son.

The anxiety, confusion and disappointment on their faces worried me a lot for years.

Andrew and I stayed in a small hotel in the Southampton town centre overnight, then in London. When I waved to them and said goodbye to Susan, Jenny and Connie, I gulped back my tears and forced a smile.

That night pretty much was as new as that first night when we married. We were lying on the bed, wondering what we should do. What surprised me was that Andrew had no underwear. Then I found his finger was empty, no more ring. His watch I gave him before he went to India, was gone. He said they were lost during the war in India.

The worst thing was that Andrew had bad stomach aches; most of the time he was in agony. That was the reason why he had been sent home from India as I was told.

The next day in London, I saw Big Ben finally, and had the famous ice cream at Lion's restaurant on Oxford Street.

Three days later, I paid five pounds twenty to buy third-class train tickets. The black *Flying Scotsman* train from London King's Cross took us to Edinburgh. Those seats were red like Noman told me. That year, I was twenty-six years old.

On that eight-hour-long journey, I looked out the window. The spring in England from what I could see, was neither warm, sunny nor green—it was chilly and grey. This country was poor and poorer than Hong Kong, I told myself, beyond all hope.

May's mother

May in her youth

May's wedding, Hong Kong, 1941

Leaving for England, 1946

A family moment, 1955

Gok & Kai in Guangzhou, 1949

Gok at work, 1951

9. Arriving in Edinburgh

9.1. She Opened Her Arms

Edinburgh is a pretty, old city. It was fortunate not to experience large-scale air raids during the war. Westward, between the dirty streets, there were rows of grey buildings with small windows. Whole areas were encompassed by them like a labyrinth: this was where the poor of Edinburgh lived.

It was almost late winter, near midnight, and drunkards shouted in the street when the noisy bars were closed. The dilapidated streets were occasionally filled with teenagers chasing and laughing around. From the box-like windows built into the grey buildings, lewd noises kept emanating from the prostitutes' homes or from the fishermen who had just returned to their wives. Everyone was so used to it, and in those paper-thin walls, no one could hide from anyone.

Among them, an unscrupulous man was roaring and a woman was crying deeply from the flat on the first floor. Someone opened the window and shouted, 'Can't you do it tomorrow? I haven't seen my woman for three fucking weeks.' The yelling didn't stop, and more violent outbursts followed—usually until the roaring man tired, and the woman fell to the ground. Their five young children were sitting next to each other, huddled on the cot in the small room, tears streaming down their faces. The second and third desperately covered their ears, while the eldest covered the youngest's while anxiously saying to the fourth, the only brother, who was sitting on the floor silently: 'You must hurry up and call the police, Father will beat our mother to death.'

'I am scared, Sarah, I dare not go out, he will kick me,' the brother said trembling, staring at the door.

'You're the only boy, be brave. You can climb down from the window, we will help you,' Sarah said.

In the dim light, the boy's terrified face could still be seen. He grabbed a bed sheet, tore off a strip of cloth and slid down while his sisters crowded onto the windowsill and looked at him fearfully.

One shoe fell in mid-air, and then the other. When he landed on the ground, he quickly retrieved his shoes, put them on, ran up the slope, turned left, and crossed the main road to the police station. He was panting hard, his face was flushed and his hair was wet. This boy who ran desperately forward was called Owen Clark Devlin, my brother-in-law. He was nine years old when I first met him in that tiny two-bedroom flat.

I hadn't forgotten what Mrs Forende said to us in Hong Kong: that if my mother-in-law hugged me with open arms the first time she met me, it meant their family liked me. I was wearing a long wool black coat, a red cardigan with a grey plaid skirt and black block-heeled leather shoes. More importantly, my hair was meticulous. My chubby mother-in-law smiled and stretched her arms out to me. She liked me, and liked me a lot all her life, really. She had dark brown, almost black hair; she was Andrew's stepmother. I called her 'Mum', just like how the Chinese call their in-laws.

'Call me Margaret, your husband calls me that,' she insisted.

Her husband, my father-in-law, went to work. He was the cook of the Caledonian Hotel at the end of Princess Street. 'Andrew's father is an amazing cook. I'm his helper, and he taught me to cook the best roast lamb which I have made for you tonight.' Margaret looked proud.

My four little sisters stood neatly behind their mother: Sarah, fourteen; Jennie, twelve; Mary, ten; and Ann, seven—they were as surprised and as delighted as I was. The skinny brother looked playful. He wore a grey coat that stretched to his knees. He gave me a sweet smile. They stared at the things I brought from Hong Kong: soda crackers, canned dace, tins of luncheon meat, dried cabbage, dried Chinese sausage, dried fish, and even Guilin chilli sauce.

This first dinner with the Devlins was the best dinner I had in a very long time. Post-war Britain was so poor that it chills me: everything needed to be rationed. One egg and three ounces of meat a week—a year without having chicken wouldn't be a surprise.

My mother-in-law's dinner table however, always had something to eat every day, whether cooked or raw, there would be some meat or vegetables—despite the shoes on her feet having almost no soles.

That evening, when I arrived in Edinburgh from London, I was so shocked to see the landlady Mrs Reagan in the shared living room. She had big white hair, her face was like a piece of white paper, and even her lips were white. Andrew explained that even money couldn't buy enough food: out there, there was nothing you could buy.

One morning, Andrew found her passed out in the kitchen and rushed her to the hospital. The doctor pricked her ten fingers but couldn't draw blood because she was so undernourished. When she got home, I saw that her hair was gone. She said the nurses shaved it to keep it from absorbing nutrients.

Mrs Reagan inherited this four-room house from her parents. She was an only child and married a doctor who died in France in World War I. Heartbroken, she started to drink until there was no more alcohol on the shelf left to be bought. She was happy to rent the largest room to a veteran and his Asian wife. She often said that she must go to Hong Kong, at least once in her life. 'The rest of the rooms upstairs are filled full of her husband's belongings. Mrs Reagan can't wait to meet you,' Andrew said about her, in his letter.

I gave her a can of lunch meat the next morning when she invited me to have tea with her. She was so delighted.

9.2. On a Snowy Sunday

I woke up early that morning, happy at the thought of Sunday lunch at my mother-in-law's house, and at my group of sisters and little brother-in-law who couldn't wait to see me.

Andrew was shaving. His cashmere cardigan that I bought for him in his size five years ago, looked too big for him.

'Darling, you look good in anything,' he said when I asked him how I looked. 'No wonder my siblings like you so much, especially Sarah. Did she teach you a lot of English?' Andrew smiled at me in the mirror.

'Yes, she did. And I like them very much,' I smiled, without telling him that Sarah had taught me how to swear in case I had to. The eldest one was always proud to introduce her Chinese sister-in-law to the people she knew. She would blush and say, 'My sister-in-law, is from Hong Kong. Do you know where Hong Kong is? A beautiful, exotic place.'

I told Andrew, 'Sarah asked me to wait for her at the school gate tomorrow afternoon. She is going to take me to a Chinese restaurant. Is there a restaurant called "Guangdong House"?

'Yes, that's the name of it. The boss should speak Cantonese. It's the first Chinese restaurant in Edinburgh. People said that it is very nice. I haven't been there.'

We decided to walk to Mother's house because it was the first snow I had seen in my life. Along the way, I was barely able to walk in my heels. I nervously wrapped around Andrew's arm.

'I'm going to buy a pair of boots tomorrow!' I shouted out while laughing.

'Yes… Wait for next week? Darling,' Andrew hesitated.

'I have money. You gave me that cheque in Hong Kong, have you forgotten?'

In fact, that cheque was never cashed. The bank in Hong Kong said that everything was now under the control of the British military and that I must ask the British military headquarters. But the British told me that they had no money in the bank. I tore it up and threw it into the sea in anger. I have never used Andrew's money in my life.

There were children playing in the snow on the street. Dressed like a rich Asian, I was often the centre of attention. Andrew always nodded and smiled to strangers. 'Hello, this is my wife, she has just come from Hong Kong.' I guess he was afraid that people would think I was Japanese.

Boys in shorts chased each other happily in the snow. A snowball hit me, and then again, wilfully. Andrew loosened my arm and turned back to those kids; he started to chase after them. He was rolling and crawling on the sliding road with his leather shoes. He looked very funny, I couldn't help laughing. I thought this *gweilo* really was a good man, worth me coming so far for.

Only a few months before, I was still worried that this man was possibly going to push me into the lake when he showed me around the landscape of Edinburgh, and then he would report to the police that his wife stumbled and drowned. She had no one in Hong Kong. Soon after, he could marry another woman who was waiting somewhere in this city. Doris May Hou, his Chinese wife, was dead to him years ago.

The kids were teasing, raising the corners of their eyes with their hands and shouting at us, calling out 'Chink, chink.'

'Darling, don't be angry. Children don't understand. It doesn't mean anything,' Andrew tried to comfort me, out of breath.

'Are they making fun of us? I asked, 'Why do they pull up their eyes?'

'No, they aren't.' Then he said, 'If someone yells like that to you again, you don't have to say anything, just hold up two fingers like this.' Andrew took off his gloves and showed me seriously: 'Remember that the back of your hand faces outwards.'

In the following years, I really did use this hand language many times, because I felt it was a secret weapon, like the swear words that Sarah taught me that I have only whispered. Of course, I have been called these kinds of words many times, not only by ignorant children.

Every time Andrew would be more angry than me, and he would scold them. Afterward, he always said that he would smash those people's faces next time. But he never did that in his life.

I told my new friend Mrs Qin, who I had just met not long ago and had come from China to accompany her husband to study medicine, how to use the secret weapon when she told me that a *gweipo* spat on her cheek on the bus and told her to go back to China. Mrs Qin cried all the way home.

'I have used it many times. It was the first sign language that my neighbour taught me. Can you believe that she is a primary school teacher,' she laughed. 'Quite powerful and easy.'

Turning around the corner, my mother-in-law's house was in front of us. We had walked for longer than usual and Sarah and Anne were already looking out the window waiting for their oldest brother and adorable big sister-in-law.

'Is Dad not at home?' I asked. I insisted on calling Andrew's father 'Dad' and he liked it. 'I want to learn how to make bread from him.'

'He's out early this morning. Doris, come and try this beef bone soup,' Margaret asked me to come over. 'Look, it's got carrots, tomatoes, potatoes, cabbage. The kids love it, especially Andrew.'

As soon as the lid of the pot was lifted, the strong smell of beef came straight out. This golden-looking soup was completely different from my Cantonese soup: thick, like shiny fatty silk. She said, 'I'll teach you how to do it. Guarantee you'll be addicted for the rest of your life.' Andrew showed us a childlike smile.

'Margaret, what happened to your face? He hit you again?' he stared suddenly at Margaret's face. 'He's hopeless.' Andrew was very angry.

'It's all my fault, I'm the one who caused it,' little Owen's face was full of guilt.

'Father came back half-drunk last night and started to scold us. He still wanted to drink. I didn't know when Owen took it to the kitchen and poured it out. I don't know why he was bold enough to do that,' Sarah began to cry. The other sisters also began to cry.

The nine-year-old flushed red and shouted: 'He would have beat Mother and kicked you if he drank again. I… I…' Tears welled up in this poor boy's eyes. It reminded me of my own father and my two younger brothers.

Andrew sat down on the chair with a helpless expression. 'If I were here, he wouldn't dare.'

Finally the old Devlin came home, carrying along a cloud of alcohol. Margaret rushed forward to help take off her husband's coat, and said fawningly, 'There is beef bone soup, your favourite.' I could see the anxiety in Margaret's eyes.

The girls were huddled together, and Owen was sitting on the chair next to me at the dinner table. It seemed he was trying hard not to be afraid. His expression was angry, and he looked to his big brother Andrew, hoping his soldier brother would say something.

Andrew didn't say a word, just stood up next to his father, picked up a large piece of bone and some vegetables from the big pot on the table and placed it heavily on his father's plate.

'What's your attitude for ? I'm your father! If it wasn't for me, you would have been given away like your sister! Would you still have married this beautiful Chinese girl?' old Devlin shouted inarticulately.

'Please don't say any more, please,' Margaret begged her husband trying to grab his hand.

'Shut up, woman!' Devlin violently shook off his wife's hand; the sharp knife in his hand flew into the air.

Margaret screamed and rushed towards the youngest, Ann, beside her.

Owen covered his head with his hands and slid under the table at once.

Andrew threw his head back on his chair.

Only I stared blankly at the knife flying through the air in an arc, which just brushed Margaret's back and fell to the wooden floor, bouncing.

The old man half-sobered up with the cries and screaming of his children.

'I'm sorry, I'm sorry, God! What shame!' He slammed the door.

I dragged Owen out, who was squatting at my feet, put my arms around him, and wiped his tears, but my own tears couldn't stop flowing. That Sunday dinner was eaten with a lot of tears. My heart sank. He reminded me of my drunk father.

That night, Andrew did his best to use his hands and feet to tell me how his father had beaten him before he joined the army. He beat him for whatever small things he did wrong as a boy. Even when he came home late after hanging around with school friends.

'Father threw his shoe at my face and yelled, '"Don't you need to go home to take care of your sister? You are useless. You should get a job, earn some money and buy your own food." I forgot my face was bleeding, I just hugged my schoolbag tightly; I was afraid that he would tear my books.'

Margaret was always begging her husband to not hit Andrew's head.

'He really didn't hit me on the head, but my legs were full of shoe prints,' Andrew said, smiling bitterly.

Such encounters did not stop until Andrew grew taller. 'I was so glad that he had to look up to me when I turned seventeen. He doesn't hit me anymore, he scolds, throws things, and hits Margaret more.' He turned to me on the bed, looked into my eyes and said seriously, 'I would never hit you, no matter what. I am not my father.'

'Don't you hate your father?' I asked.

'I can't hate him. I pity him more. He was telling the truth; if not for him, I would still be in Ireland somewhere. Wouldn't have met you, and so no Mrs Doris Devlin.'

Yes, Andrew had never even raised one finger to me, but one thing he had inherited was his father's appetite for drinking.

In Andrew's earliest memories, his father was always a man with a mouth smelling of alcohol and a red face. When his father came home, as soon as he heard the sound of the lock and key opening the door, his back would get cold. He didn't know whether his father was tired and emotional that day. Frequently he was worse for liquor, which made him surly, and Andrew the oldest was always the target; the next, Margaret.

Andrew's birth mother was Norwegian. She worked in Andrew's grandfather's small bar in Ireland. Soon, she got pregnant with the pub owner's young son without getting married. She gave birth to two children—Andrew and his older sister.

When Andrew was only two years old, his mother died of illness. From then on his father started drinking heavily. Andrew and his sisters had suffered a lot, often beaten by their drunk father, until one day, when his father drank his grandfather's best bottle of whisky and smashed all the pots and bowls in the kitchen, his grandfather drove him out of the pub with a dirty mop.

The young Devlin came to Edinburgh looking for a living. He got a job in the Caledonian Station Hotel. He started to fancy his new assistant, the kind and capable Margaret. He married her and had children with her. When his oldest son Andrew came to Edinburgh to join his new family, he was ten years old.

Andrew said when he walked into his father's home, Margaret also embraced him with open arms. His sister was left in Ireland. I've never met her.

Joining the army was Andrew's own idea. 'It was like I went on holiday with friends in Asia, to a place with hot sun and odd foods, and then—those dainty and cute Hong Kong girls,' Andrew said slyly.

What I was thinking was that if it wasn't for his father, Andrew, whose handwriting was as neat as a print, would have gotten a decent job in Edinburgh, he might not have joined the army and left home for the Far East.

As the Chinese say: 'A good man won't be a soldier; good iron won't be a nail.' But it is so wrong. Both my husband Andrew and my brother Gok were good men.

9.3 My Boss Married a *Gweipo*

The first Chinese restaurant in Edinburgh was called the 'Guangdong House', it had started its journey before the war.

I was the first Chinese waitress in the Guangdong House because I could speak English.

The owner of the Guangdong House was forty-year-old Mr Wang. He was working for the Blue Funnel Line, once one of the world's well-known shipping companies, owned by a British company called Taikou. It was the most important eastern shipping company which linked European trade with China. He was a boiler fireman, the toughest job on the ship. One day, he got off the ship and never wanted to go back on it.

Initially, he was a shoeshine boy, then a doorman for a hotel. There was a Scottish girl waitressing in the hotel. They married, and Lulu became Mrs Wang. A few years later, Mr and Mrs Wang bought a four-storey building on Chambers Street.

They set their home on the second floor; the restaurant was on the first floor; the kitchen was on the ground floor, and the staff's accommodation was on the lower ground floor, which was also a storage area. The top floor's three rooms were rented out to six students who came from China and Hong Kong. When dinner time came, someone beat the copper gong in the hallway, like in the Chinese opera.

Mr Wang proudly named his restaurant the 'Guangdong House', after the province he came from.

One day, Mrs Wang couldn't find her husband. She asked everyone in the restaurant. She went to the casino where Mr Wang was a regular, to ask around until eventually she went to the police station to report her husband missing.

'Your husband is in Cindy's home,' a kitchen assistant told her. Cindy, who had yellow hair, was a widow of the vegetable shop's owner where Mr Wang got his cabbages and carrots from.

Two days later, during a busy lunchtime, Mr Wang tried to sneak onto the second floor to collect his things. Mrs Wang saw him and she grabbed the largest cabbage from the kitchen and shouted words I had never heard before. She held it over her head with two hands and threw it at her husband with all the strength she could while screaming at him. Mr Wang with one hand covering up his head, the other carrying his luggage, ran out and shouted at the end of the road: 'Lulu, the restaurant is yours now. I want children, you can't give them to me.'

Mrs Wang sat on the street and cried despondently. I stood beside her and looked at her husband as he drove away. I felt more sad for Mrs Wang than anger at Mr Wang.

I picked up the cabbage which could have made a lot of chicken chop suey. Probably enough for a busy lunch. At that time, for three shillings, you could have chicken vegetable soup, stir-fry chicken with vegetables, and one bowl of boiled rice. One chicken could make twelve pounds worth of business.

This happened after only five months of working for them.

The first time I went to the Guangdong House for dinner, was with Sarah. She said, 'My English teacher has been before. She told us the crispy rolls called "spring rolls" are the best.' Sarah looked excited.

That night, Sarah ate two portions of spring rolls, twelve in total. Mr Wang was extremely pleased to see me. As was Mrs Wang. They kept bringing out a lot of dishes which were only cooked for staff: steamed chicken feet in black bean sauce, and slow-cooked pig feet with ginger and sweet vinegar.

Mrs Wang reached over with her chopsticks to replenish a big piece of pig feet in my bowl.

'This certainly is one of my favourites. My husband said according to Chinese tradition they are the best food for women to eat after giving birth,' she smiled, 'but I eat it every week.'

Soon after, I started my first job in England: a waitress in the Guangdong House.

Every day, I walked from home to get there at eleven o'clock, put the gas fires on, mopped the floor, took down all the chairs from the tables, used boiling water to warm up the plates and gave them a good wrapping with towels. Those eighteen tables and fifty seats were mine mainly, to run for lunch.

I earned five pounds a week plus tips. I made more money than Andrew, who was a civil service clerk for the City of Edinburgh Council, and earned about five pounds a week.

I was also the secretary for Mr Wang and his Chinese kitchen staff and for some of their friends in Edinburgh. I wrote them letters to send home and read them the letters they received from far away. Those letters were from their farmer parents or siblings; some of the letters were from girls who their mothers thought were suitable for their sons to marry. Most were telling of the hard life in the poor villages and asking for money to be sent home. Their happiness and sadness, I knew it all.

A man called Yang, his letters told me he was getting married in his village. But instead of him, it was a rooster acting as a groom with his new wife to do all the wedding ceremonies. The rooster would be held by someone acting as the groom, to kneel and bow in front of ancestors of the ancestral hall, and also bow to the bride who he had never met.

The marriage was arranged by both parents like most others. Since then the bride loosened her braids and tied up her hair into a bun at the back; she stayed in his home as the daughter-in-law and waited for her husband to return home one day—it could be for years.

Apart from sending money home, the letters he asked me to write for him were the same: 'Don't worry about me, I am good. Look after Father and Mother. Hope to be home soon.' But up until I left the Guangdong House, I didn't see Yang leave Edinburgh for China.

Since Mr Wang left, poor Mrs Wang's drinking became heavier. Almost every day she was drunk. The next day she couldn't even get out of bed. I'd keep her lunch in the steamer for her till the afternoon.

Mrs Wang begged Andrew and me to move into her flat on the second floor. We were given the largest room. 'You now, as my children, no rent. I am pleased you and your husband are staying with me,' Mrs Wang said emotionally.

The business had gone down since the cooks came and went without Mr Wang in charge of the kitchen. More and more jobs started to land on my shoulders. Andrew would help when I was waitressing by myself sometimes at the weekend. The stress began to fill up in my chest.

9.4. Going Back to Hong Kong

It was the third Christmas coming for me in Edinburgh. Snowflakes fell outside on the street. Like every Christmas, Edinburgh tried its best to create a happy time after the war. But it didn't clear those dark clouds gathering in my heart and overhead.

This city was still a strange place to me; I didn't know who the man was whose sculpture was on Princes Street. I was still a stranger to the people of this city, who always asked me for my passport to prove I was a citizen because only citizens could buy things—even when I handed over my ration book.

I felt alone and gradually became unhappier day by day. The worst thing was that I had no sign of pregnancy. We had tried hard and hoped intently. I had visited different doctors and had done different tests. I drank a lot of Chinese herbal medicines which were sent to me by Pauline from Hong Kong.

'Don't be feeling gloomy and disheartened, darling, a baby will come,' Andrew would say often.

'What if it doesn't? Andrew,' I said, 'if we were paying a little attention eight years ago in Hong Kong, our baby would be in school by now.'

I couldn't help but think the reason I could not have a child was because of my sins; my body wasn't clean enough for a child to grow, it had been invaded by the devil and my womb was stained filthy. I suffered from insomnia and crying without reason. My emotional turmoil drained me.

On one of the worst mornings, I thought I was dying because I felt I couldn't move and I couldn't even breathe. The doctor said to me finally, 'Go back to Hong Kong, Doris, you will feel as if you have never been ill. Trust me.'

In January 1950, I decided to leave. It was a quick decision. Andrew did not hesitate and resigned the next day from his job.

'Marry a dog, then I must follow that dog; marry a chicken, then I must follow that chicken—you are my dog and chicken, so what I should I do?' he looked at me and said primly. I couldn't help but laugh. This man was a fast learner, and he did love me.

On the *Queen Mary*, Deck 5 in Room B340, without a balcony, I slept tight.

Andrew confessed on the first night on the *Queen Mary* that he was engaged to a Scottish girl after he was told I had died. He sold his wedding ring and the watch and bought her a diamond ring. It was he who called off the engagement when he received a letter to confirm I was alive in Hong Kong. He chose to leave her heartbroken.

'She married an Irish man and moved to Dublin. She has a son and another on the way. She seems happy, I hope so, really.' Andrew was trying to smile, but couldn't hide his guilt in his eyes.

I didn't tell him about Sang and Norman, never did. I guess I was protecting both of us.

But I had felt that this *gweilo* husband was the man who I would spend my life with, no matter what.

I sat down on a chair on the deck, under the warm sun, and on a small table started writing to my brothers and Pauline telling them I was coming back to Hong Kong.

My dearest friend Pauline got married seven months before. It was a surprise when I received Pauline's letter. She married a British Navy officer John Shaw, who had been a Japanese prisoner for more than three years in Sham Shui Po, where Pauline and I threw the bread over the wire fence once. John chose to stay in Hong Kong and became a police officer like some of the veterans.

Pauline was wearing a white wedding dress and standing beside a strong man who was in uniform. She looked proud. My wedding gift to Pauline was a green jade bracelet with a gold clasp, I bought it as part of my own wedding dowry. I knew Pauline would love it.

The most important thing was knowing my brothers could come to Hong Kong to be with me soon. I finally fulfilled my promise to have a home for us that I had tried so hard to make happen.

I looked at Gok's photo he sent to me. My handsome brother was in military uniform, his blaster was slumped low, and he wore it in a leather black gun belt. Around him were his colleagues, also in uniform. They looked in high and vigorous spirits. Gok was still a soldier, he had joined the People's Liberation Army of the Communist Party. He was posted to Pan Yu, a county-level city belonging to a region in Guangdong. He was appointed mayor of the largest town.

I liked to stand at the stern aft when Andrew went for drinks, to see the waving sea drift away from me. I felt like I was leaving this far, faraway place for home. My fate, which the blind woman had predicted, wasn't coming true.

Looking up to the sky, I couldn't help but smile. Our good days were coming.

Postscript

Norman

On a sunny day, a year after we were separated in Southampton Port, Norman suddenly walked into the Guangdong House restaurant. I was just carrying four dishes kicking the kitchen door open, and the chicken chop suey almost fell. Norman was wearing a suit, his hair carefully combed with wax. If it wasn't for his smile and voice, he was nearly unrecognisable.

'Doris.' He was standing in the doorway, his burst of brightness and exuberance almost overwhelmed me at that moment. But following, I was in a spin.

I asked him to sit down and ran to the kitchen to ask for a stir-fried shredded chicken with cabbage for Norman and made a pot of green tea for him. That lunch seemed like a particularly long shift for me, with Norman sitting quietly eating, his eyes following me between the tables and the kitchen.

'Mrs Forende wrote to me, she said that you are working in a restaurant.' As soon as I walked with Norman out of the restaurant door, Norman stopped in front of me and couldn't wait to ask, 'Why didn't you tell me that your husband left you? Why didn't you call me, Doris?' He came to find me because he thought Andrew didn't want me anymore and I had to work for a living.

I took him to the cinema, I forgot what movie it was. Then, I walked him to the train station. I was worried I would be seen with a man, a stranger, together by someone who knew me.

'Please don't come to me again Norman. Find a girl to marry and have children,' I told him. I didn't tell him that the shilling he asked me to keep, I still kept in my drawer somewhere.

Again, Norman didn't say anything else. He stared at me for a little while, then said, 'I didn't say goodbye to you that day in Southampton. I'm saying goodbye now. Goodbye Doris.' His eyes were glistening with tears.

Just before he boarded the train, he asked suddenly, 'I have a few shillings, can I give it you Doris?' I shook my head, 'No more Norman, go home'.

To travel back to Wales, Norman had to change trains twice and the bus three times.

Since then I haven't heard anything from him. I regret that I didn't tell him that only a week before, the restaurant cook caught his hand in the pasta maker, dripping with blood. I jumped into a car, and dropped him to the emergency room of the hospital. The cook said to everyone that my parking was perfect.

'My friend Norman taught me in Hong Kong,' I said proudly.

Mrs Forende

With huge regret, the painting of a blind man playing erhu was lost, as well as Mrs Forende's photo.

In her black and white photo, behind her smiling face, there were a lot of paintings on the wall in her London home. 'To my little darling Doris. July 1946,' she wrote down on the back of the photo.

Two years later, I received her letter from London: it said that she had stopped drinking wine, only coffee now. She also said that she was going to Israel to join her husband to fight for their land. That was the last time I heard from her.

I have always thought Mrs Forende was a British spy. I don't know why. No matter who she was really, she was always my first, unforgettable, *gweipo* friend.

Dr Clarke

The last time I heard from Dr Clarke was in 1975, he sent me a book with a letter. On the bright red cover, I recognised him straight away. He was seated in the front row, holding a ceremonial rod, a bit younger but the smile was the same, a very English gentlemanly look.

'My dear Doris, everything is passing by so quickly. I hope that you and your husband are well. This book is my memoir of my work, part of it was in Hong Kong. It may help Andrew understand what you have gone through.' He wrote with very tidy handwriting.

He died March 13th 1976 as Sir Selwyn Selwyn-Clarke. A man, a hero to me, in those dark days of Hong Kong being occupied by the Japanese, he had done so many things for the internees and the prisoners of war, including for those wives, children, widows and orphans. I could never forget him.

Connie

Connie left her husband because he didn't love her any more. It was his mistake. He said he shouldn't have accepted her mother's gold ring. But he was going to keep their sons if she wanted him to. Connie shouted at him—if he wanted their sons then he must keep her too.

She moved out with her sons and rented a tiny flat in Chinatown. She found a job as a restaurant cashier.

She signed the divorce papers and intentionally brought it back to her husband's flat. She wanted to throw it on her husband's face. A woman opened the door.

'She has chestnut hair, light blue eyes, very pretty and polite. I must say,' Connie wrote in her letter, 'I didn't throw the paper, I was so discouraged.'

Connie brought up her sons very well on her own. They became decent men. It's said April showers bring May flowers.

'When people see my older son, they don't believe I am his mother; when they see the younger one, they don't believe his father is English—that is very annoying,' Connie said.

Sometimes she would come to Edinburgh to see me, her old friend. Connie was proud, although she had worked very hard as far as I could see—her hair was all grey and her back was stooped down. 'Who said it would be easy? You don't have to tell people. You aren't special.' That's her phrase.

Susan

I came to Liverpool to visit Susan once. She was waiting for me at Lime Street train station. She trotted toward me quickly when she saw me getting off the train.

I hugged my old friend. Shy little Lily gave me a big smile when I showed her my gift—a pink dress doll with blinking, twinkle-blue eyes.

Susan was coughing non-stop. She told me she had a cold for quite a while. 'You need to see a doctor, Sue,' I said, looking at her pale face.

'The foreigners' medicine isn't good. I have some herbs, it helps.'

We went to Chinatown, which is the oldest Chinatown in Europe.

'The Wang's restaurant is a place I was planning to come with you. I have heard they do very good soy sauce chicken, just like those in Hong Kong. ' Susan showed she was so looking forward to it.

'How are you doing, Susan?' I picked up a chicken wing to place in her bowl; I knew that was her favourite.

Susan didn't look at me and said, 'What could I expect, Doris? He isn't at home often. Once I followed him. I saw him entering a house. There is a woman with brown hair. He has the keys.'

'What are you going to do?' I was worried.

'I don't know. I didn't say anything. What can I say? My money has all run out. I want to go back to Hong Kong, with Lily.'

I actually had the same thought at the time. But I said to her, 'Look at your Lily now, when she is grown up, you are going to have good days.'

'Yes, she is my only hope,' Susan smiled. 'You know she has started to like potatoes more than rice.'

'Mama, the deep-fried chips are the best,' Lily said biting a large chicken drumstick, 'but I still like soy sauce chicken very much. I haven't eaten it for quite a long time.'

'Oh, you are having it now,' Susan said, stroking her daughter's hair, 'are you sure you don't want to eat this steamed salty fish with minced pork?' Susan pointed to the white metal plate.

'No, Mama,' Lily shook her head, 'Grandma said if I eat it I will smell like dead fish. No one will come near me at school.'

'My mother-in-law tried to stop me from eating those salty fish. I eat it in my room when I want to. But I have eaten them all now. I can only have it when I go back to Hong Kong. One day, and I hope soon.' Susan seemed cheekily happy, unlike her.

That night I slept in Susan and Lily's room on Susan's camphor trunk with a chair supporting my feet. The whole house smelled of tobacco. I didn't see Susan's husband. Only her mother-in-law.

At midnight, I heard someone climbing in through the living room window. 'It is my husband. Doris, go back to sleep,' Susan waved her hand.

The next day, I asked Susan's mother-in-law for Susan and Lily's rations.

'She has no money, what are they going to buy?' this woman, sitting in an armchair with cigarettes in her fingers, said sneeringly.

'I have money. Those rations belong to Susan and Lily,' I insisted.

In the train station, Susan hugged me tight and said, 'Doris, I am so envious of you. You are strong. Andrew loves you, admires you and respects you. Me… I wish I had listened to my father's admonishing when I married him.'

A few months later, I received a letter from Liverpool. Inside this brown envelope, there was a pearl necklace. It belonged to Susan; she wore it all the time. The letter was written by Susan's husband. Only a few words—Susan had died. She wanted me to have her necklace for remembrance.

My heart went to Lily immediately. I wrote back to him to ask about her. I said if he didn't want Lily, I would take her to Edinburgh and raise her like my own.

But I never heard from them again.

My dear friend Susan died of lung cancer aged twenty-six, after one and a half years living in England. I always couldn't help but look out at those girls on the street who had a Chinese and English face, hoping that I may see Lily again, and tell her about her mother Susan.

Jenny

Pretty and lovable Jenny had committed suicide. She wrote to me a letter before she died.

In London, on the third day after Jenny's arrival, her husband told her that war was over, he just wanted a calm life and she should as well. He had been with someone else now, an English girl. He had asked Jenny to go back to Hong Kong.

'Sometimes I wish I got pregnant with him before he was sent away from Hong Kong, it may have made things different,' Jenny said when we were on our way to England. Thinking back, she must have sensed that her husband had changed. But she still couldn't stop hoping.

Her last letter I received, had been bathed in tears. Some words I was unable to read. All I could see was Jenny sitting in front of an old desk, crying out the pain of her broken heart in silence—only tears. Her final words were: 'We will meet again, my dear friend Doris.'

Holding that piece of paper, it felt like heavy metal in my hand, full of grief. I had to sit down and was unable to speak.

Beautiful Jenny jumped into the River Thames to her death on a spring sunset evening.

She must have been wearing her favourite dress—silk ivory with navy blue borders around the hem. Simple, pure, just like her soul.

10. Irresistible Destiny

10.1. That Girl

She could never understand that old woman in the little village, who after only listening to her mother read out the day and the time she was born in that dark room, moved her eyes, both covered by white film and gave her mother a message of prophecy for her five-year-old daughter. She wondered if she was born one day earlier or half a day later; or even if on the same day, if she was born one hour earlier or even one minute later—would she still be on that ship?

The old woman's prediction sadly in fact was just like a silent curse, still sleeping. It would wake up to haunt that girl.

The ship left the Hong Kong pier on an evening in December 1962. It was going to be at sea for days.

The five-year-old girl on it, was now forty-four years of age, a wife and a mother. This time there was no return from the far, far away: England. She knew she really couldn't escape and she had to accept her destiny.

'Have you had your medicine, Andrew?' I asked, tidying up my husband's blanket.

'Yes, darling with my tea.' Under the warm sunlight on the Indian Ocean, Andrew smiled. His chair made a sound when his heavy body moved. His hand was shaking constantly. He was unable to control it. We sat at the aft, looking steadily out to the horizon. I was getting farther away from my home and was getting closer and closer to the place of the blind woman's prediction.

'Mama, my stomach feels funny again.' My adorable eleven-year-old daughter Astrid came over from the other side of the deck where she was skipping rope with some other children.

'I told you don't move too much.'

I let her sit down on my chair and used my favourite Chinese medicine secret weapon, white flower oil, to massage her temples and held the little bottle under her nose. She was wearing a dark green checked dress I made with the famous Scottish tweed. A faint camphor wood fragrance emanated from her dress in the air; she always said to me, the smell she did not like.

I knelt between them, wishing that this big ship would arrive on the shore of Edinburgh as soon as possible because Andrew was ill.

Twelve good years in Hong Kong had gone by quickly without even my noticing.

Just two weeks after I was back in Hong Kong in 1950, my brothers arrived. When I saw them both walking out of the train carriage at the station then, twelve years before, both of them were in the prime of their lives. On the contrary, I had become old in their eyes.

Gok was choking. 'My sister, you are getting old…'

Kai just grinned and stood aside quietly, he held an old, not big, suitcase tightly in his hands. Inside was all he had.

We only spent two weeks happily together in my home. Gok was determined to return to the mainland. He was going to forge a new China with the Communist Party. He had no plans to stay in Hong Kong.

Gok said to me, that his brother-in-law was a good man. He would listen to me and would not bully me; he felt hugely relieved. 'I told Andrew that he looks like a Buddha, but he doesn't understand. I don't know how to describe it to him in English, you can explain it to him,' Gok laughed. It was such a relief to know my brothers liked Andrew although they couldn't communicate. Gok promised to come back to Hong Kong to visit us soon, he even had a plan that he was going to start a chicken farm in Hong Kong when he came back.

Soon, Kai started to work in a tailor shop in Hong Kong Island. He lived in the shop.

Not for long, the new Government of China started implementing border management, and a Hong Kong restricted border had formed, ninety-one kilometres in length. There was barbed wire, dogs, rivers and soldiers. The free movement between the mainland and Hong Kong had ended. Smuggling became the only way enter to Hong Kong from the mainland.

It was too late to give my brothers a home as I promised—this became what I regretted the most when I lived in Hong Kong.

Pauline, who became Mrs Shaw, was always just there; she came and went, following the life trajectory of the both of us. None of us could get rid of anyone. It seemed that it was destined and couldn't be resisted.

Sang was married and had two sons. He worked for the hospital as an ambulance paramedic. We didn't meet again intentionally, nor by chance. Looking upon a sea of faces on the busy streets, I sometimes hoped I could find his face. But I didn't. Our encounter was like the wind blowing through time.

He died of throat cancer in 1962. For the rest of my life, I would rather believe he was still alive than know he wasn't there anymore. He was the man I loved the most from the bottom of my heart, I couldn't deny that. Although it's hard to believe, even myself, that we had never even held hands.

Our new home was a stone-built house at Diamond Hill, Kowloon. We were the first tenants to move into one of the three nearby similar houses. The last family that moved into the biggest one was Mr and Mrs Collaco, who came from Portugal with their two sons. Mrs Collaco later became my newborn daughter's godmother, and I became the godmother of her eldest son Ivan's new wife, her daughter-in-law Lorna. I never thought that the eighteen-year-old Lorna would become the most powerful wife in Hong Kong one day.

10.2. Bruce Lee's Mother Was My Mahjong Player

I was enjoying the privileges of a wife of a *gweilo* police officer in Hong Kong. For example, I could eat and visit some places that were only for British or white people. And I was the mother of a mixed-race, beautiful, more Western-looking daughter, who was holding hands with her tall, handsome and well-dressed father walking beside me. Sometimes a nanny was following. I won the attention and respect of all the friends around me. I swelled with pride by living above most of the Chinese in Hong Kong at that time.

My daily routine was playing mahjong and making friends; most of them were Cantonese opera actors, even film directors. They were looked up to and loved by Hong Kong people because the fifties and sixties were the golden years of Cantonese opera. They were often sitting around my mahjong table and gossiping about Hong Kong.

The mahjong game was developed in 19th century China, beginning as a game for wealthy people. It has spread throughout the world since the early 20th century; anyone can play for fun but it is mostly played for money—the excitement of gambling, with skill, strategy and luck. Someone described the essence of mahjong as creating and ordering out of the chaos on the base of drawing from those tiles randomly.

People say that wherever there is cooking smoke, there is a Chinese. I say there is a Chinese wherever there is a mahjong game.

The people who you sat with around the mahjong table showed your societal status and your friendship circle. After hours and hours of playing, listening to the gossiping and gossiping, everyone knew everyone's secrets in the excitement and enthusiasm.

At that time in Hong Kong, playing mahjong to gamble was illegal if you didn't have a licence.

One day, I was playing at a friend's flat. The building had just been investigated by police, who were looking for illegal mahjong gambling activities.

'Do you know who her husband is?' one of the players drawled, pointing to me when Chinese police officers wanted to impound our mahjong.

'Sergeant Devlin,' Mrs Lee said. The beautiful Eurasian Mrs Lee was the mother of Bruce Lee. She gave the officer a cheeky look. 'Do you know him?' And Mrs Lee insisted she would not move away from the mahjong table. She had the looks of Eurasian ancestry. Those two poor Chinese police officers had to leave us with empty hands. Following that, I gained a reputation: having me sitting around a mahjong table would make it a safe place to play.

Friends came along with their friends. Amongst them was a famous Hong Kong Cantonese opera actor and film director, screenwriter Wong Hok Sing who made two hundred films. He even helped to change my baby daughter's nappies when the women were too busy playing mahjong.

I took a commission from my mahjong players; sometimes I had two tables of mahjong players at home. I was making a good income, I did not need to find a manufacturing job. Every day, I could have decent food on my dinner table; my daughter could have piano lessons and went to a good school with a nanny. It was far better than my neighbours Jimmy and Susie. They had to borrow money at the end of every month. During the 1950s, a police officer was taking home about three hundred and fifty Hong Kong dollars a month. It certainly was not enough for a family of four.

A lot of corruption in the Hong Kong police force wasn't surprising during that time, until the establishment of the Independent Commission Against Corruption by Governor Sir Murray MacLehose in 1974. I always made sure Andrew wasn't one of those people.

Miss Yuk was one of the biggest Cantonese opera stars. She was also around my mahjong table often. She was a top-notch player who I always liked to play with because she giggled happily when she won, but was not annoyed when she lost the game. I was envious of her voice, bright and smooth, no matter whether she was acting as a young girl, deeply in love, or a heroic woman—when she opened her mouth to sing, the audience would be amazed. I could have the best seats in the theatre while everyone else fought for them. Of course, I wouldn't forget to send a huge basket of flowers backstage to congratulate her on a successful performance.

The famous Miss Yuk had seven children. 'Every one is your bone-melting dragon,' she always said. She meant they would absorb you, rip you apart and consume you when bringing them up. And she really had been. Because when she sat in front of the mirror and applied her makeup in the room backstage, she couldn't find her lips. She had to use her finger to find her lips to colour them. Her lips were as pale as her face.

'May, I think you are much better than me,' she said to me more than once. 'Your husband always obeys you, even sitting down when you insist on playing mahjong after arriving home from work. Poor him, yesterday, he was falling asleep when he was playing. Look May, marrying a *gweilo* isn't always a bad choice I think, truly.'

Although, there was a secret between us—the debts she owed me. I didn't mind lending her money so many times to help her get through those hard times. I realised that they were the people dressed gorgeously on the stage, but their unknown hardships behind the scenes, were sometimes downright tragic. Not what the young May had imagined.

It was no secret that Mrs Lee was an abandoned baby who was luckily adopted by a wealthy and decent family: Sir Ho Dong's half-brother and his mistress. But, as she said sometimes, 'Whatever, I am still an adopted daughter who came from nowhere.' It made me think that was the reason why she ended up in troupes and married an actor.

And her son—named 'Little Dragon Lee' wasn't Bruce Lee yet, he was still a troublemaking teenager who was forced to learn kung fu by his father, a famous clown in the Hong Kong

Cantonese opera. It was quite normal to hear Mrs Lee complaining about her son, 'I don't understand why this boy, born in the year of the dragon, is becoming like a monkey.'

'I knew he would be a naughty boy when I helped the delivery. He cried like a knocked gong in the opera,' Yuk shook her head grimly.

We all laughed.

Whatever we joked about Little Dragon Lee, a dragon or monkey or a knocked gong, we had never thought he would become the Bruce Lee, an icon all over the world years later. I have always thought that since Bruce Lee became widely known, the Chinese endured less racism on the street. Some people like to believe all Chinese can use kung fu to fight. Even if they just made sounds like those from kung fu, they could still scare off those troublemakers.

I also learned to smoke from them—I could be like my dear friend Mrs Forende: taking a drag then holding it for a bit, the long smoke drawing out from my mouth, circling, and disappearing in the air. My nails were in red. Cigarette nipped between my index and middle fingers.

10.3. Pauline as Mrs Shaw

'It's so good to have you back, May,' were Pauline's first words when we met again; we hugged each other in tears. 'At least I don't have to pay someone to write you letters and read your letters, and also I don't have to send you those medicinal herbs to Edinburgh anymore,' she added.

'Is your husband good to you?' I asked, staring at the three deep wrinkles on her and holding her cracked hands.

Despite Pauline never being able to pronounce her surname correctly, she started to drink English tea, with a nice teapot and a cup on a saucer. 'Where are your tea bags, are they Lipton?' she asked when she walked straight to my kitchen, like she normally did. 'I must have a cup of milk tea. The green tea upsets my stomach.' Pauline was drinking her tea nicely, with her little finger raised up.

Then, she and John adopted a five-year-old girl from an orphanage and named her Debra without telling me.

'When the adoption isn't ensured, how can I let you worry May? How nice your Astrid has a companion now, like us.' Pauline had her reasons all the time.

The first time I met little Debra was in my home.

'My daughter, Debra,' Pauline was grinning at me, 'Come, this is your Aunty Doris.' A skinny shy pretty Western-looking girl. 'Aunty Doris,' her voice was almost inaudible. It made me think of Susan's daughter Lily.

Debra's mother was a wealthy family's daughter who fell in love with an American businessman. She had been pregnant for three months, when the American told her that he must go back to America to make some arrangements for her to move to the US. But he didn't come back until the baby was due.

Debra's mother secretly gave birth, and left the baby with someone to look after her and went to America to look for her man. But no one saw her again in Hong Kong. That someone had to send the only six-month-old Debra to an orphanage. Pauline took her home.

Pauline said with a sigh despondently, 'I wish I could have adopted her earlier. Now she is old enough to know I am not her real mother.'

She added, 'May, I think I'm still lucky to have John willing to marry me and that he doesn't hate me and that I have no children to give birth to, although he sometimes will beat me after drinking too much—but men are all the same: they get drunk and go crazy. Don't they?' said Pauline tearfully. 'Once, I could have had my little pilot, but now... I don't know why my stomach just can't get bigger anymore.'

When I met John finally, I wished his gruff exterior concealed a good heart. But, I saw him kick over a street stall, and the poor old Chinese man, picking up his oranges which had fallen everywhere, was bowing his back saying sorry.

'Sir, sir, my oranges are very sweet, try some, try some,' the old man handed over a few oranges to John. Pauline put them in her bag, then holding her husband's arm, walked away superciliously.

'We'd better keep some distance from them, darling,' Andrew advised me. I could not agree with him more.

Also, because our social circle became different, the closest friendship between Pauline and me drifted away gradually until one trivial matter happened and we stopped talking for more than two years.

It was at our daughter's fifth birthday party. John smacked Astrid's face. Astrid knocked her head on the corner of a coffee table, hard.

The reason was because Astrid grabbed her toy rabbit that eight-year-old Debra was playing with, and Debra cried very loudly.

'Beat her, penny pincher,' Pauline was comforting her Debra and signalled her husband to do so. No one in the room thought this big man would do it.

One day I suddenly received a phone call from Pauline. She cried in despair, 'May, May, what am I going to do? May, you tell me, John died, how can we live on without him?'

On that morning, Pauline found her husband still sitting in a chair outside the balcony with his head down; he was drinking after late duty the night before. Without an answer, Pauline nudged his shoulder, and his stiff, heavy body fell on the floor with a grey face.

I put everything down and went to her.

Poor Pauline had to go back to her old job—laundry and ironing. Then, she became a partner in the laundry shop she worked for. Her life with her daughter was ongoing. We were back to what used to be, sister-like lifelong friends.

While Pauline had good days, my bad days were more and more to come because of Andrew's illness.

10.4. Andrew's Illness

It started with little things, like dropping his pens and being unable to hold his chopsticks properly; sometimes he fell from his bicycle on his night patrol. Then, he would stagger when he walked into the living room. And then, in the bed, with me.

The doctor told us it may be caused by Andrew's heavy drinking. Yes, Andrew did drink a lot. Especially at weekends, those Western police officers loved to drink and chat in their own pubs all day long.

Once I went to look for Andrew. One of his colleagues laughed at me and said, 'Mrs Devlin, you better handcuff your husband—I can lend you a pair.'

I thought it may be caused by drinking the water I boiled in a large copper pot. Andrew himself believed it was caused by a serious injury when he was a boy.

'My left thigh had been plunged into by a rusty sharp point of a metal garden fence,' he told me. 'I snuck into someone's garden with my friends, we were just stealing some apples from the tree. We had been chased after by an old man from the house. I was in the hospital for one week. Look now, what a mess.'

Actually, no one knew the cause. But I knew he was getting worse and worse. I kept it as secret as possible. My worries were hidden very well behind my smiles every day.

Andrew was diagnosed with Parkinson's disease six years after he followed me back to Hong Kong from Edinburgh. His boss kindly moved Andrew from the front line to the police department headquarters as a clerk to do what jobs he could manage until Andrew had worked long enough to get his pension. He said, 'That is what I can do for you. You need to go back to Edinburgh. They have the best treatment for your disease. We have contacted the veterans association in Edinburgh, they will look after you.'

Again, Pauline burst into tears when I told her we must leave Hong Kong and wouldn't be back this time.

She gave me a red box: a very nice green jade pendant with a gold necklace which was similar to the one I gave to her as my gift for her wedding.

She was weeping, 'May, do you know that you are the only family I have left? I am going to follow you to Edinburgh. Would you promise me and Debra, May, would you?'

'I would do it when I settle down. We are sisters.' I promised her.

10.5. Goodbye Hong Kong

The heaviest feeling was to tell my brothers that their sister would not be coming back to Hong Kong this time.

In the tea room opposite Kai's workplace, he sat and listened quietly without asking any questions. Then he stood up. I stuffed three hundred Hong Kong dollars into his hand and told him to find a girl to marry. He grabbed the money and left without looking back. When looking at my thirty-eight-year-old little brother's back, my tears were flowing down, he was getting old.

In the past years, Kai spent his day trampling the sewing machine in the small shop; at night it was his place to sleep. The large fabric-cutting table was his bed. He didn't have a home.

Gok's life was destabilising with the political factors of the communist party in China.

As I knew, the nice colour from being a member of the anti-Japanese had faded on my brother. Gok found he was no longer welcome to join the Communist Party, which was the only condition you needed to fulfil to get promotions in your career. No matter how hard he tried: following orders, sacrificing any personal interests—he buried himself at work for years, but his underlings were promoted one by one, and only he was demoted year after year. Finally, the government found an opportunity to remove his job and sent him to rural areas in order to help the farmers to do land reform.

They called this the 'Revolutionary Action of Land Registration.' This meant taking land from wealthy landlords and giving it to those who had nothing. Those landlords were kicked out of their homes. Their belongings suddenly all became somebody else's who everyone else thought they deserved. All deeds you owned were burned in a fire.

'I am glad that our family had nothing left before 1949. Otherwise, I would have been classified as a landlord or a capitalist. I would have been criticised and denounced by those angry people. I probably would have been executed by shooting, or have been put into jail,' Gok wrote to me.

Gok was classified as a vendor because he sold pickled olives and owned a rooster stall, but not as a poor and lower-middle class peasant or as the working class, who were trusted members of the Communist Party. People were treated differently depending on their classification. The worst classification was that of the landlords and big capitalists.

Gok's career had been limited by his vendor identity. 'I am a person who needs to try very consciously to change. I must reshape my mind. I must study Chairman's Mao theory seriously,' he also wrote.

I didn't know what was in my brother's mind. But I respected what he believed in as long as it kept him safe. I was only hoping for him to return to the city where life would be much easier.

One thing happened that caused Gok to be delayed in returning to the city from the land registration job he had done for two years. Young and handsome Gok had fallen in love with a colleague, an ambitious girl.

Gok couldn't wait to write her a letter, asking her if they could take the relationship one step forward beyond comradeship. Gok folded his letter into a bowknot beautifully and placed it inside Chairman Mao's red book. After a night studying Chairman Mao's theory, as he did every day, Gok gave the book to this girl. I guess that night, Gok must have had no sleep, because it was his then first and only love.

The next day, Gok had been called upon by the commander to his office. He displayed the letter on the table and said gravely, 'Comrade Hou, do you know what you have done is very serious? You have gone against the rules. Everyone here must do their job with undivided attention and not allow personal feelings to be expressed. Tonight you will self-criticise in the night meeting.'

That night, Gok read aloud his written self-criticism shamefully in the meeting. Everyone, including the girl, criticised Gok. She said Comrade Hou had disturbed her from doing her most important job, and that fortunately, she had strong political awareness and didn't fall into his trap.

The girl was praised. Soon she was sent back to the city and given a good job. Gok had been lowered in the rankings as a member of the capitalist class, whose mind needed to be seriously reshaped and reformed. When everyone else who was sent to the village at the same time as Gok was posted back to the city, Gok instead had to stay for another year and a half.

Since then, I haven't heard that Gok has been in love with anyone else. He must have been hurt deeply and fearful of being in love again. That was the 1950s.

At that time was one of three great refugee waves from the People's Republic of China to Hong Kong in history. It was caused by floods and famine, hungry civilians and political class struggle. It impacted students, intellectuals, soldiers, and those who were previously wealthy. During this dangerous time, people were risking their lives trying to smuggle into Hong Kong. Large numbers of people died, bitten by sharks, drowning, jumping off trains, or being killed and injured by either the Chinese Communist Army or the British Army.

I couldn't forget what Yuk told us: 'My two cousins were nearly fed to the sharks, luckily a large truck tyre saved them. One year of learning how to swim better had paid off. Then, they hid in the mountain waiting for dark. But they still got caught—lucky again: they were *gweilos* without a dog. The luckiest thing was that they gave my name to the interpreter. And you know what? They let them go and told them how to get to the theatre to find me.'

My heart sank. I was worried Gok would do the same, despite my hoping he would come back to Hong Kong. I even repeatedly drummed into Andrew to remember his brother-in-law's name and appearance, and also let his fellows know about him.

In 1963, three days before I left Hong Kong, I received a letter from Gok with a photo. A young woman with short hair was sitting beside Gok smiling. 'To dear Sister: my wife and your brother,' Gok wrote on the back.

Gok's wife was a primary school teacher who was divorced and had a three-year-old son. About two years later, Gok had a son. He called him Fei. It meant 'flying'. Gok was forty-one years old.

Only Pauline and my goddaughter Lorna came to port to see us off. Kai didn't come. Everything seemed deserted and hopeless.

10.6. Settle in the City I Want to Avoid

That voyage was smoother than it had ever been before. A flock of seagulls were hovering over the deck looking for food. They must have come from those unknown little islands. I looked at the waves rolling up and falling back hard to dark water. Hong Kong was getting further and further away.

Finally, we saw Mrs Wang who was waiting for us at the Port of Leith in Edinburgh.

'Oh dear,' she said. 'Andrew has gotten worse than what you described in your letters. Not good Doris, really.'

'He will be better after the surgery. The Edinburgh hospital has the best experts for Parkinson's disease,' I told her in the front seat, 'they have arranged a bed for him.' I could see the stress hidden in Mrs Wang's wrinkles; how could there be no wrinkles on my face? I thought.

When our car stopped outside the Guangdong House, I was staring at it this time with intent. It looked an utter far cry away from how it looked twelve years ago, during the good days. I was worried that it would be difficult for Andrew to climb to the second floor where Mrs Wang kindly offered to let us stay.

Our daughter was sent to St Margaret's Conference school, an expensive private girls boarding school which I believed was best for her. I believed that no male run school would cultivate a ladylike temperament for my daughter. Because I couldn't do it myself, not to mention her father was seriously ill, and needed my care.

I started to look for a house to buy. I found a beautiful Georgian terraced townhouse in Fingal Place, right by Meadows Park. Following the elegant curved stone staircase to the first floor where there were four bedrooms, there was a large vaulted glass roof where you could look up to the sky. The cast-iron railing was sound, and could be used safely for Andrew to hold onto. Andrew could take a nice walk in the park and even on his worst days, whether Andrew was in the bedroom or the living room, he could see the green through those large windows. I did all the fresh painting and bought all the furniture.

'Darling, this is a beautiful house.' Andrew couldn't hide his excitement when he walked in the first time. 'When I am sitting by the window, I can look out to the park, and I can take a walk.'

I smiled, it was just as I thought. It was reassuring to see Andrew's hands were shaking less than before the surgery.

We moved in the 1963 summer, the most beautiful season of Meadows Park. As green as Hong Kong's spring, and as warm as Hong Kong's autumn—that was what Andrew said to me. When Andrew asked where the money came from, I told him from the apartment we sold in Hong Kong and I had sold my favourite yellow diamond and some gold jewellery, and from some money from the bank—they called it a mortgage.

For me, it was the first time that I heard of a mortgage, and I wasn't aware that after eight years, I would still owe one thousand two hundred pounds to the bank for borrowing one thousand five hundred. Since then, I never borrowed any money from those banks again.

Andrew was in and out of hospital. I worked for Mrs Wang even though she signed a paper with two of her waitresses as witnesses which transferred the possession of the Guangdong House under my name. 'You must take over this place, you are the only person who can run it,' she begged me. 'This place is my life.'

At that time, her ex-husband had two children with Cindy. They had moved to Glasgow, opened a restaurant and were doing very well.

'I don't want the Guangdong House to be closed down, I don't want them laughing at me.' Mrs Wang wept.

After all those years, Mrs Wang kept her surname and did not change the name of the restaurant named by her ex-husband, because her heart was still set on Mr Wang years after she was betrayed and deserted.

That was how I suddenly became the owner of the Guangdong House. But, I had never seen myself as the owner of the Guangdong House. I left one and a half years later. Guangdong House then changed hands twice, but could not survive from finally closing down. The first Chinese restaurant came to an end. Mrs Wang died soon after.

10.7. The Tea Room on Clerk Street

My restaurant, the fourth Chinese restaurant in Edinburgh, was finally opened at the end of the year, December 1963, and at the end of the month, December 29th. My little dream was standing at Clerk Street. I called it the 'China Garden'.

Nine months before, I was still a waitress who was waiting for the bus outside this four-storey building. Bus number seven would take me to my friend Mrs Chan's restaurant, The Golden Crown, the third Chinese restaurant in Edinburgh. Some days I helped her at tea time after I finished my lunch shift in the Guangdong House.

The bus wasn't on time, as usual. My stomach started to gripe again. I walked into the little coffee shop just behind the bus stop, as usual.

The stomach aches began when Andrew was sent to the hospital for his operation, and when my daughter kept begging me not to board at school, as did Andrew. He said, 'Let Astrid stay home, she could help you and look after me.'

'I don't want her to go through what we are going through, and what I went through when I was her age,' I said firmly. I didn't tell him another important reason was that I didn't feel safe for my daughter who had gradually grown up into a mature and pretty young girl. There were too many men around her that we couldn't protect her from.

Meanwhile, letters came one after the other from Pauline, with one main message: when could she and Debra come to Edinburgh; the sooner the better—because she had left the laundry business and packed up her luggage. Pauline insisted on coming to Edinburgh to be with me, no matter whether I agreed with it or not.

Pauline and her daughter Debra arrived in Edinburgh six months later. I arranged for them to live on the top floor of the Guangdong House for free, and gave her a job in the kitchen so they could have free meals and accommodation.

On a Wednesday afternoon, I shouted upstairs, 'Pauline, Debra, dinner time!'

But there wasn't an answer.

'They moved out this morning Doris,' a waitress told me, 'Pauline asked everyone not to tell you. I helped her buy a house. I am very sorry.'

Pauline bought a nine-bedroom house. She was worried I was going to ask her for a loan to buy my house because she knew I was short of money.

I sat down on the chair and looked at the salty fish steamed belly pork which was Pauline's favourite dish. I lost all my appetite. Since then, my stomach aches came even more often and worse.

Drunk Mrs Wang looked at me with a long sigh, 'I did say to you that you are stupid.'

Since then we hardly saw each other for a few years despite us living in a small city. But we knew what was going on between us because the Chinese community was really small.

But Pauline was Pauline. She was always there, just coming and going, whenever she wanted.

The little coffee shop called 'Clerks Tearoom', had a narrow ground floor and narrow wooden stairs to the lower ground floor kitchen. Whenever looking at this little place, I wondered if I could one day own it. I thought when people went to the cinema just across the street they must look for something to eat before and after. That would make for a booming restaurant.

Surprisingly one day the owner told me, 'Doris, we are selling the place, I know you are interested. Talk to my solicitor.'

He gave me his solicitor's name and also gave me another solicitor's address and said, 'You need a good solicitor. He is one.'

It was Marwick Solicitors on Dundas Street. He became the only solicitor I ever used. I bought Clerks Tearoom for four thousand pounds.

I never knew I would have to face so many things. The restaurant licence officer came and said the kitchen ceiling was too low, the only option was to dig into the ground to make it high enough for a normal human to stand up in. Otherwise, they wouldn't give me the licence. Digging down was the only option. It cost three thousand pounds extra. And with those builders who came late, left early, and never missed a tea time break, it had taken five months longer. This meant my restaurant couldn't open before Christmas.

'If I had fifty pounds to please my wife, she would let me work every day,' said the painter. I gave him the money, which was almost the last of my savings. The next day I waited and waited for him to come, to finish painting the ceiling. But I never saw him again.

That night, I went home at midnight, my hair and my face covered with white paint. 'Darling, you look like a panda,' Andrew tried to get up from bed. 'Ben and Tai cooked chicken wings in oyster sauce, nearly as good as yours.'

Ben was my waiter, Tai was my cook. They had been living in my house for five months waiting for the China Garden to be opened. I needed to pay them their salaries as normal to keep them from being snatched by other restaurant owners. For Ben it was five pounds a week as a head waiter; Tai was paid nine pounds.

Like I did every day, I wrung the towel from the warm water, wiped Andrew's face and neck, helped him sit up, and wiped his back and front, then his bottom.

'Darling, the hospital said they can send someone else to help me if we don't like that carer,' Andrew said.

'No, Andrew, they didn't look after you well, otherwise your bottom wouldn't have two large bedsores.'

'Astrid does very well, she even washed me like the nurse did.' Andrew suggested tentatively, 'She wants to stay home; she wants to help you and me.'

'I can manage,' I was avoiding Andrew's eyes, I was even more determined that Astrid must stay on boarding. I would stick to my plan no matter how hard, I told myself.

I changed the hot water bottle and put it inside his quilt. 'The restaurant will open this weekend, no need to be worried about it. Go to sleep.'

It was not until one o'clock in the morning that I lay down on my bed in the next room. Andrew and I started to sleep in different beds since Andrew had his operation. Now it was in different rooms. We never slept together again. I was in my early forties.

In the dark, I stared at the ceiling, which was so high. I thought of what the doctor told us, that Andrew's surgery was a new medical treatment for Parkinson's disease; they believed there was light ahead for Andrew.

'Holes have been drilled into my head,' Andrew told me when he woke up in hospital. He truly believed he could be back to being a husband and father as usual soon after; he thought he maybe could play football with his veteran team soon. Hope seemed ahead for us, but I doubted it when the quivering became shaking again.

That night I actually had no sleep.

11. Running the China Garden

11.1. My Cook Ran Away

My China Garden was opened at all 'ends'. End of the year, end of the month—such bad *feng shui.* I wasn't surprised that now it was at the bottom of the rankings of the Chinese restaurant businesses, I always joked with my dear friend Mrs Chan, who with her husband ran their restaurant. They had a booming business for years. Her three sons had private school education from age four.

'We are not much better, Doris,' Mrs Chan tried to console me as always. 'Don't forget you are on your own. I admire you for working so hard. Have you found your new cook yet?'

Looking for a cook was the most inordinate nightmare for me because I was determined to have a good cook, but I couldn't pay more.

One rare Saturday, it was busy. My only cook, who famously had a unique character, could be very angry if it was a busy day. Halfway through cooking a beef in satay sauce, he suddenly just threw the wok on the cooker, and walked out of the kitchen. He disappeared through the back door.

I chased after him outside to the street and begged him to come back.

'Did I do something wrong?' I asked.

'You never told me it would be that busy,' he said. 'By the way, can you cook? You can't. Why are women running a restaurant and I'm not? I will come for wages tomorrow.' He drove away.

A woman's helpless feeling had never been as strongly surged in my heart as at that moment. I forced myself to swallow my tears.

'The boss of the new restaurant offered him more pay last Saturday when they played mahjong together,' his assistant told me.

I rushed upstairs.

'I am so sorry, your order of stuffed duck has sold out; duck with green pepper in black beans is nice, do you want to try?' I asked table two with a smile.

'I am so sorry, the scallops aren't very fresh, I can't give them to you. Would you like instead king prawns, which I got this morning in the market?' I suggested to table five.

Then I rushed down to the kitchen, picked up the wok to cook that beef satay sauce first, then rolled up my sleeves and cooked the rest of the meals. I truly didn't know what I cooked, but I didn't get any complaints.

I was quite sure that I was the only boss in Edinburgh who was always anxiously worrying that their cook wouldn't show up on the Sunday after Saturday payday. Because only if you could cook, would you have the power to sack the cook if he overslept two hours late for work because he was playing mahjong last night; or could you refuse to pay him next week's wages in advance, because his money had gone to the casino tables on his payday.

I found my own ways to still see them in my kitchen every Sunday.

I would very carefully ask the cook to re-cook meals which were brought back from the customers. 'This is a very demanding *gweilo* who likes a stronger taste, just give him more salt if you don't mind.' Even though I knew he probably forgot to put salt in while he was talking about his horse-betting elatedly.

Apart from that, I opened the mahjong table and called some people to come to my restaurant after closing—no matter how tired I was, and how much I wanted to go home to be with Andrew. Playing mahjong with them seemed a good way to keep my cooks and the staff from being snatched by other restaurant owners.

Therefore, my daughter called her mother a mahjong addict; my face looked grey, and my clothes and hair reeked of tobacco smoke mixed with the smell of the kitchen cooking oil smoke.

She said she hated mahjong since she had memories of her mother and her friends being so busy playing, seeming to forget she was sitting in the room and crying. It was no surprise that my daughter never wanted to play mahjong, unlike everyone else.

'Take Astrid away, quick, would you?' her mother waved her hand to the nanny.

Astrid hated people smoking too, she could smell tobacco three days after someone had smoked in our house because she couldn't forget how the living room in Hong Kong was smoky all the time, that her mother had her own ashtray and it was always more full than everybody else's. Her clothes smelled of tobacco her school friends told her, it was disgusting, and her piano teacher said that as well when he put his hands on her skirt.

It followed I always needed to be sure I had as little smell as possible when Astrid was home during half-terms in her nine years at posh St Margaret's.

11.2. Professor Moore

The customers who pushed open the small glass doors of the China Garden were a variety of people, including doctors and professors from the nearby Edinburgh Medical College. Some ordinary families came from the cinema opposite us. There were also various reasons to walk in; filling the stomach was just one small reason among many.

In the beginning, at first, people wanted to come and see what the smallest Chinese restaurant in town looked like; second, people wanted to taste if there was any difference from the others, hoping that this one would be better suited to them than their own. Since then, some people I saw again; some others would come back almost every week, ordering the same dish for many years which became part of their lives. I called them my favourite regulars. They came not because my sweet and sour chicken was particularly delicious, nor because it was more comfortable to sit in my narrow restaurant. They were just kind to me and they knew that I insisted on getting fresh meat and fresh vegetables by myself, leaving an ill husband and getting up early to go to the market. Professor Moore and his wife were two of those regulars.

Mr Moore had done profound research on Chinese culture and had been to China and Hong Kong many times to study and teach. They always shared a portion of spring rolls as a starter and the husband would order beef chop suey; the wife, sweet and sour chicken, and they would order one big bowl of Yangzhou fried rice to share with the meal.

'There is no such kind of fried rice in Yangzhou as this,' said Mrs Moore, 'and there is no sweet and sour chicken balls, but sweet and sour pork, which is half fat. The Chinese are smart to know how to alternate for the English.'

'Give me a real Hong Kong-style soy sauce chicken, would you Doris?' sometimes Mr Moore would laugh, 'like those hanging inside the windows, with the skin and ass on.'

On the kind Mr Moore's high recommendation, the China Garden received its biggest of business opportunity, which was cooking for about fifty people who came from all over the world for a medical school conference.

I spent two weeks preparing.

I went to their canteen kitchen with three of my staff, cooked a lot of sweet and sour chicken, deep-fried a lot of spring rolls and made bowls of Yangzhou fried rice; I even cooked lots of toffee apples for dessert. We made sure everyone was very happy.

'It's truly delicious, everyone said so, Doris,' Professor Moore came into the kitchen and gave us a thumbs up, shaking the only man's hand, 'Thank you very much, excellent cooking.'

Actually, this man wasn't my cook, he was the man who chopped vegetables and meats in the kitchen. My cook had left two weeks ago.

Of course, I couldn't tell Professor Moore that it was me who cooked that evening. I was proud.

On the way home, I thought if I could cook for a few more conferences like that one each year, I could pay all my bills and have some money left in my pocket.

Two weeks later, I received a letter from the university medical school department. In addition to praising the China Garden's delicious food, it criticised us for not being safe and forgetting to turn off the gas stove, which almost caused a serious accident.

The professor and his wife hadn't been since.

11.3. James, the Young Police Officer

When your doors were open on Clerk Street, you couldn't avoid people who aside from filling their hunger, were also willing to take some advantage of you—especially those people who had a few drinks from the pubs nearby. They probably thought I was just a Chinese woman and on my own. I was afraid of them walking in, and angry with those picking on me when they were out of their minds sometimes. This happened during those days in the city, and still did.

I was lucky it only happened to me once. That night when the door was about to close, two men swaggered in with a strong smell of alcohol.

'Salt and pepper pork ribs, deep-fried won tons, Peking duck with pancakes—and give me duck breast, not the bottom bit,' one of them shouted inarticulately, without having to look at the menu.

'I want special fried noodles and special fried rice,' added the other. One just slumped down on that table. It seemed that they were very familiar with Chinese cuisine.

'Don't you think it's too much for only two?' I said carefully, because I didn't expect they would pay the bill and I could stand to lose less. I was trying not to panic and didn't forget to signal my waitress to go to the downstairs kitchen and tell the men we having trouble.

Just as I was about to take the order down to the kitchen, two police officers came in. They walked to the two men directly and asked them to leave.

'They are troublemakers. My boss saw them walking into your restaurant, he called us to help. You must be Mrs Devlin. Your husband was a police officer in Hong Kong, am I right?' one of the new and young officers, James said. He clearly had a Chinese-looking face.

After that, James showed his face in the China Garden quite often. Maybe that was the reason my restaurant had less trouble than other Chinese restaurants.

James' father was Chinese and worked for a shipping company in Liverpool. They shipped silk, cotton and tea from Shanghai and Hong Kong to Liverpool. During World War II the ships carried munitions, voyaging on dangerous seas; his father alongside other Chinese men worked very hard below deck in the engine room. His mother was an English girl from Liverpool who met his father Hua in a dry cleaning shop near the dock.

'He was wearing a suit with a black wool felt hat, and his hair was waxed tidy. My mother told me that,' James said. James' mother married Hua happily and had children, he was the youngest and the only son among four children.

Before a normal working trip to Shanghai, James' father told his wife he was going to buy a gold necklace engraved with lucky words for his newborn son when he arrived in Shanghai.

But he never came back.

A few years later, James' mother moved to Glasgow to be with her sister. She never married again. She believed her husband wouldn't have left her and their children just like that, something must have happened. Because it wasn't just her Chinese seaman husband who didn't come back, all those working on that same ship also all disappeared.

Throughout 1945-1946, hundreds of Chinese seamen were put on ships and sent back to China by the police and immigration inspectorate in Liverpool (those working with the shipping companies). The English wives of the men and their children were never told what was happening, never given a chance to object, and never given a chance to say goodbye. Most of them believed their husbands, their fathers, had abandoned them.

James' mother did everything she could to persuade him to study hard in school because it was his father's wish.

'He said, "A boy must go to school, he must become a decent man,"' James said. James didn't go to college because his mother was ill. Then he became a police officer. 'A decent man, just as my father wished,' James smiled.

'I don't have any memories about him and we don't even know where in China he came from,' James told me. 'My sisters told me that he was a very good cook. When he was home, he would cook something odd, but it tasted nice. He soaked the beef into dark soy sauce and left it to dry by the fire. He put it in a big jar as a snack—but only if you were being good.' I could see the light in James' black eyes.

I had joked with James that he should go to Hong Kong, so he could find soy sauce dried beef as good as his father's. He could join the Hong Kong police and meet a Chinese girl to marry.

When I retired from the China Garden, I received a wooden plaque, written in gold. This beautiful plaque was from the Edinburgh Police—the institution Andrew was affiliated with during his lifetime. James was the person who presented it to me in my restaurant.

I liked what he said: 'You deserve it, Doris.' It was quite an honour for me.

I didn't tell James about that young boy, a boy I still thought of, because I didn't know who should get the blame. It was the same boy who always rushed into the restaurant after school when he passed by. He pulled up his eyes and shouted, 'Chink, Chink', again and again, for days.

Bennett, my part-time student waiter, was very angry. He was determined to give him a big lesson. On a Friday afternoon, Bennett hid behind the door and waited for him.

The boy showed up again on time.

Just before he was going to do the same thing again, Bennett dragged him to the kitchen downstairs. He put the boy's head on the big chopping board, picked up a kitchen knife and shouted: 'You think this is funny? If you do it again, I will chop your head off. Do you hear me?'

Bennett chopped the knife on the board very hard. The boy's face looked white and startled. Since then we hadn't seen this boy again. I hope he was alright.

And Bennett wasn't even Chinese. He was a Burmese who was sent to Edinburgh to study by his wealthy father.

Despite saying often that he didn't like England and would not be interested in *gweipo*, it turned out he married a beautiful Scottish girl, and settled in Edinburgh for many years.

11.4. Mr and Mrs Mill

I stopped the car in front of the traffic light, and an Indian woman in a headscarf dragged three children across the road hurriedly, for fear of the waiting cars on both sides.

'I don't know why there are so many immigrants. They look so unfit in this country. Shouldn't they go back to their own country for good?' Mrs Ella Mill sitting next to me frowned. 'Ah, haha, I didn't mean you, Doris, you aren't the same.'

I didn't speak, nor look at her. If my husband wasn't Scottish, would she still be my friend? Would she still want to travel to China with me? Sometimes I couldn't help but think about it. But Ella had been my close friend for many years.

It was lunchtime, only a few customers.

When I walked into the kitchen, my cook said while cooking, 'Boss, I saw a mouse walking around this morning. I said hello to the little thing and he stared at me for a moment, then disappeared.'

I was frightened to death, mostly worried that the mouse had gone upstairs in the restaurant—maybe it was hiding under the table, hanging around customers' feet.

'I looked closely and couldn't see any holes it could hide in,' my waiter Ben said, while he was holding up a whole lunch set meal passing through the kitchen door.

'It mostly goes into the storage room. It's only a little one, less than half the size of the mice in my home town, it's no big deal. No need to panic.' My cook wiped his sweat with the towel that was always on his shoulder. A forty-year-old man who still couldn't find a wife, he was certainly a good cook, but just wasn't tidy and clean enough.

I hurriedly instructed Lucy, my English waitress, to call the Health Department immediately to report it.

'Are you crazy Doris? They will close the restaurant,' she looked shocked.

Mr Mill from the Health Department came after lunchtime. Sure enough, some sand was found on the lower ground floor in the storage room, and a small hole led to the candy store behind the wall.

'I have to go to their store and pull the floor up to check,' Mr Mill said.

'Please don't go,' I replied quickly, 'I don't want to cause any trouble with our next door. Can you advise me how I should stop the mice coming through?' I begged.

'Give me an empty beer bottle,' Mr Mill called to Lucy, who was watching the excitement.

Mr Mill grabbed a table towel, wrapped up the bottle, and placed it on the table, 'Give me a hammer,' he said. There was no hammer. I handed him a large kitchen knife.

Mr Mill, a gentleman, tall and well-dressed, lifted his hand and smashed the towelled bottle into pieces. He put the shards of glasses into the small hole carefully.

No more mice were seen. I didn't know if those mice were still living next door.

Mr Mill didn't order me to close my restaurant. Instead, he became the biggest helper of my restaurant business for years after. He would even help my friends' restaurant businesses when they had trouble. I realised that there were always good people who tried to help in this country.

Mr Mill's wife, the cheerful Mrs Ella Mill, also became my friend too.

Every Christmas, I bought a turkey for everyone who helped me to get through that year. I thought it was a way to show my appreciation. Mr and Mrs Mill were on the top of my list.

The first year, I gave a red paper envelope with fifty pounds of lucky money inside to Mr Mill, along with a turkey. Ella chased after me to the bus stop, gave me a hug and a large box of chocolates, and returned the red paper envelope.

They were honest people with integrity. I didn't mind that she sometimes forgot that I was Chinese, and an immigrant. She was a real person, who spoke her mind.

Ella ran a B&B a few streets away from my restaurant. One evening, she took a big brown envelope, shoved it into my hand, and said hurriedly, 'Doris, keep it for me. I am going out with my husband for dinner. I'll pick it up tomorrow night, it is just some cash.' Only then did I realise that you could earn so much money by opening a hotel. My restaurant only did two to three hundred pounds of business a week, and there was not much left after paying the staff and the bills and taxes.

Mr and Mrs Mill used to live in Cape Town, South Africa.

'South Africa is a very special place; we enjoyed a lifestyle with first-class treatment, even if you had nothing in the UK,' Mrs Mill said with pride. 'They were the happiest days of my life, just the two of us.'

Those were good days for white people in the sixties to seventies until they were endangered when black people started to attack them.

'We were stuck at home for weeks. Ran out of food and water. All the white people were scared to get out of the metal gates of their home areas. The shouting and the gunshots came one after another,' Ella said. 'I called Charles, who was working for Nelson Mandela's people, to help. He refused.' Charles was the son of Ella's housekeeper.

'I paid his school fees and gave clothes, shoes, and food to his family—even his name was given to him by me. He had a good education and then got a good job.' Disappointment and sadness overflowed her face. 'He had the power to ask people to let us go through the checkpoint and go to the European Army base. Did you know? Doris, the two of us were going to be shot and killed by the black people if they broke through the iron gate. I wrote a note to my son saying I was sorry I left him in Edinburgh,' Ella said in a choked voice.

'You know who saved us from danger?' Ella broke into smiles. 'A Chinese man, a plastic factory engineer from Taiwan. He was my neighbour's friend's friend. We hid in his truck, covered by boxes and black plastic bags, just like the movies,' Ella laughed. 'Poor man, he risked his life to do this, he said he was actually very scared—he almost wet himself when he passed the gate roadblock where the gunman was standing.' Now I could see why Ella and her husband were friendly to me and the Chinese.

At that time, Ella's only son had stayed at an Edinburgh boys' boarding school.

'I lied to the school about my son's age. They only accepted boys from seven years old. But he was only a few months younger,' Ella said. 'I couldn't forget his tears and how he cried.'

I met Ella's son a few times. He became a solicitor before he moved to Sydney.

Ella asked me, 'Do you think I should go with my son to Australia, Doris?'

'Leaving your husband? No, Ella.' To me that was unthinkable.

But Ella chose her son over her husband. She sold her business and went to Sydney and soon, bought a house for her son.

One day, I received a letter sent from Ella, '…I am living in the downstairs bedroom in the house where my son is staying with his new girlfriend. To be honest, I do have a little regret that I didn't take your advice. I wasn't allowed to use the telephone to call my husband and I'm not allowed go to upstairs without asking…'

A few years later, Ella's son went to New York, and she followed him. She was treated the same way by her son and his New Yorker girlfriend.

I guessed Ella wanted to make up for lost time with her only son. It was too late, clearly.

Ella finally came back to Edinburgh because her husband died and her son moved to Thailand and married a Thai girl. They refused to let Ella go to Thailand.

'I have met my son's wife. A lovely Thai girl.' Ella looked happy and old and weak. 'I am going to leave all my inheritance to her, the Eastern people are more credible and honest—I am sure she will look after my son.'

I was speechless for her naivety, I thought truly.

I visited Ella a few times while she was staying in a luxury nursing home in the early eighties. But I never heard of her son and her daughter-in-law having been to see her.

The last time I saw her was in the nursing home garden. Under the afternoon sun, her grey hair was almost white.

'Doris, I think we made the same mistake: we should have not sent our children to boarding school. Didn't we?' She looked at me in my eyes.

'For better or for worse, we have done it, Ella, but we felt it was better for them, didn't we?'

'Did Astrid quit her job to move to Canada?' Ella asked with a smile.

'I hope not Ella, but her boss is going to keep her position for her when she comes back from Canada. It means she has done a good job in that hospital.' I was proud to tell Ella and also worried my daughter wouldn't come back.

Since Astrid graduated from college, she started to work for the Royal Edinburgh Hospital, as a secretary. She wore a skirt, heeled leather shoes, lipstick, and spoke posh English. She was good at her job, a decent lady just like I wished.

'What a sweet girl Astrid is, you taught her well when she was young—at least she has those traditional Chinese family values which respect the older generations,' Ella said with a bitter smile.' I still remember when we got lost in the streets when we travelled to China—she kept saying that my mother would be worried to death. She was so panicked.'

It was 1974, an unforgettable trip to China. I remember Ella showed me a sketch of a rooster in a Beijing hotel and said, 'What a surprise, Doris, Astrid has an amazing artistic talent. Where does she get the talent from? What a waste. She should go to art school, not a secretary course.'

'She probably ends up drawing on the street begging for pennies one day if I let her study art,' I tried to say casually. In fact, I was starting to worry. She once showed me her painting—a mother and daughter with no clothes; they looked lost and lonely.

12. Gok, China Garden and Andrew

12.1. Sitting in a Red Chair with My Brother

The China trip Ella talked about was a group trip organised by Mr Lui, who was the head of the Chinese community: the 'China Voice'. It took me almost a year to complete preparations, including all of mine and Andrew's personal details, and especially Astrid and Ella's who were both going to travel with us. They were obviously the most excited. To me, after those years of waiting, it was so good to be able to meet my brother and his family.

Astrid had to provide a guarantee document by her employer, as did Ella, which were her solicitor and me. On the China side, Gok was the person who would happily receive me. He was examined repeatedly, and he had to guarantee my personality to be that of a 'good person'.

I received a strange letter of invitation from my brother:

> *Dear Sister: Welcome back to China during your busy schedule. Under the leadership of Chairman Mao and the Communist Party of China, the motherland has undergone earth-shaking changes. We have all lived a good life, and the hard days under the old party have long passed. Our whole family is very happy to know that you will be back, and we look forward to seeing you and niece Astrid soon.*

At the end of the letter, Gok especially added: '*Please buy my son Fei a good radio.*' Only this and the last sentence, were what I believed Gok wanted to say.

It was a long flight from Edinburgh to London to Beijing. In Autumn, our group all wore navy blue uniforms with gold and red badges embroidered on the front pockets, including Ella and my twenty-four-year-old daughter. We all felt very proud because we were treated like important people. Wherever our coach went, there would be police motorcycles at the front, and cars following at the rear. If it was necessary, their cars would flash and sirens would blare. We had an interpreter and our guide Miss Ling sent by the consulate who spoke English, Mandarin and Cantonese. I shared a room with her. Astrid and Ella in another.

During the last night in Beijing, my sore throat was still not getting better. I was unable to speak properly. The reception girl cooked fresh fish congee with herbs at home, filled it into a thermos bottle, and brought it to my room. She knocked on my door at night.

She looked around with alarm when she told me that her mother cooked this congee, which was good for a sore throat. Her mother was from Guangzhou and spoke Cantonese. She also asked me to keep quiet because she wasn't allowed to contact overseas visitors personally.

'Oh, some visitors?' Miss Ling asked, when she was back from a meeting and saw the thermos bottle on the table, 'What is this for?'

'Oh, I asked the receptionist to bring me some congee. You know I can hardly swallow food.'

'I didn't know that you could speak Mandarin, Doris,' she peeped smiling, and walked into the bathroom.

'I wrote it down on paper,' I raised my voice.

'Oh, yes, I forgot about that. No worries, Doris. She was kind.'

The next morning, I gave a cashmere cardigan to Miss Ling. 'This is warmer—for our visit to the Yuan Ming Yuan Old Summer Palace tomorrow. Your clothes aren't warm enough, it's chilly outside the city. This cardigan was made in Scotland.'

'Oh, how beautiful! Thank you so much Doris.'

Miss Ling of course knew that it was Scottish cashmere, which is the best. I never saw her wearing my brown cashmere for the rest of those days on the trip. But I found things went more smoothly, specifically meeting my brother in Guangzhou.

'Bless her, Miss Ling,' I wrote to Andrew in a letter I had to address to the hospital during our trip to China. 'We have arranged to meet my brother tomorrow. Astrid is excited to meet her uncle and his family for the first time. Did you tell the nurse to cut off the fatty bits from the bacon? Broccoli is good for you.'

That was also the first time Andrew and I were apart from each other for so long and for such a distance. I wrote him despite my letter probably arriving after I returned home.

Finally, we were in Guangzhou where we would meet Gok. It was the last city on our trip. We arranged to stay in one of the best hotels called the Overseas Chinese Mansion, which stood beautifully by the Pearl River. It wasn't open to the public. It was a privilege to have a room or have a meal inside.

Poor Ella finally had bread with butter for her dinner for the first time on this two-week trip. She said, 'Doris, I never knew that bread could be done so nice; it looks so soft, so tasty. If I toast it, it will be perfect.'

Helpful Miss Ling asked for a toaster. The handsome manager took the bread to the kitchen and came out with slices of barbecue-smoked bread which I believed they did with a wok.

'This is the best toast I have ever had,' Ella gave him a thumbs up with a big grin. From then on, Ella ate her barbecue-smoked bread every day until she flew back to Edinburgh.

On the last evening in the Overseas Chinese Mansion Hotel, Ella and Astrid decided to take a walk along the Pearl Riverbank after dinner.

'Just cross the road, don't go too far away please,' Miss Ling advised them. 'Your Western looks will attract people's attention, believe me.'

They were gone for much longer. It was getting dark. I was starting to worry.

'There is no need, Doris, we will take care of it,' Miss Ling told me.

Two hours later, Mrs Mill and Miss Devlin were sent back to the hotel in a luxurious black car. It turned out they got lost in the side streets of the riverbank. Astrid asked for the way back to the hotel in Cantonese, but people answered her in English which she didn't understand. Then, a car pulled over quietly, and an un-uniformed man walked to them and invited them to get in. They introduced themselves as police.

'Mysterious, like James Bond, Doris,' Ella sounded excited. 'I am glad I came to China with you,' she winked exaggeratedly.

On Ella's last day, when she was packing her things in the room, I was eagerly waiting to meet my brother Gok, whom I hadn't seen for twenty-four years since that summer of 1950. Ella insisted on meeting my brother and his family. Miss Ling said to her, caring and firm: 'Mrs Mill, you don't have time for that. We will send you to the airport one hour early, don't stress yourself, please.'

In a large conference room on the hotel's ground floor, I finally saw Gok with his wife and their nine-year-old son, Fei.

Gok had lost more than half of his hair. He wore a blue suit, the same as the other men I saw on the streets. It was spring, warm, but his buttons were done up to his neck.

We were both holding back tears and gripped our hands together. I was so sure that he would have cried if there weren't two strangers sitting in the corner, holding notebooks and pens.

'Don't ask things you shouldn't ask,' Miss Ling had warned me kindly last night.

Before my brother was allowed to come to see me, he was invited to a meeting by the Public Security Bureau. He was told directly by the police what should not be said and what should be said.

We were seated primly side by side in huge red armchairs. We talked like strangers because I didn't know what to say and how to talk with my brother, who looked so nervous.

'Are you used to the weather, Sister?' Gok asked with a broken voice. 'Oh, Astrid, the Wen Nan tea I sent to you was good?' He turned to Astrid, who was seated in another armchair, looking so confused in that atmosphere, with two men sitting next to her, their heads lowered, always writing. Astrid stared at me with a blank expression on her face and nodded her head. She tried to relax.

Miss Ling walked into the room and suggested, 'Why not take a look at the lovely garden?'

It was only when we were allowed to walk in the garden, that the nervousness released a bit; even though those two men were following, they kept their distance.

I felt like the cashmere wasn't enough, I should have given Miss Ling my fur coat to show my appreciation for the exceptional arrangement she had managed for us.

My only nephew was a shy boy who had very bright eyes and big ears like his father. He held Gok's hand and listened.

'Do you want to go to England to study?' I asked him, trying to lighten the atmosphere for the first time we met.

'No, I don't,' he replied.

'He will study here,' my brother's wife stepped forward and said desperately.

After only about one hour, we were told the meeting was finished. We took a photo together with my camera. It was one of those two men, who held the camera for us.

He said, 'Nice camera. Made in Japan.'

Gok had to leave. They weren't allowed to stay for lunch as I wished.

It was an extremely stifling acquaintance. Sadness and helplessness filled my heart when I saw them walk out of the security gates, and when Gok turned back to wave his hand, he looked old and small; I seemed to have seen an eleven-year-old him waving at the road of our village home.

Years after, my brother explained to me that during that time he was being watched as a politically untrustworthy right-wing person. He was one of the people in the 'Five Black Categories'—he was a traitor.

Following the tragic Cultural Revolution in the 1960s, the May 7th Cadre School began. Mao ordered the re-education of cadres and intellectuals in proper socialist thought. A lot of people were sent to these labour camps to do hard agricultural work where they studied Mao's theories. These 'schools' were located in poor and remote rural areas. Among them were cadres of the party and government staff classified as capitalists, scientific-technological teachers of universities and colleges, and reactionary academic authorities. This included people like Gok who was untrustworthy according to the Communist Party, and those people who were well educated but wouldn't keep their mouths shut, or those who wouldn't get on well with those in power.

They were called capitalists, traitors, spies, right-wing, etcetera—those that Mao believed would threaten his power. They could be senior or young, they could be sent by themselves or with their entire families. They could be the weak, the sick or disabled people. They were organised according to the military establishment and lived a militarised life.

Every day, they had to shout out slogans and sing Mao's quotes when they went to work and after they finished work. This work some of them had never done before: farming, picking up manure, raising pigs, fetching water, digging wells, and building houses for themselves to live in. A lot of them were overwhelmed and died of diseases caused by overwork and torture.

Gok was classified as a traitor to the Communist Party because he had betrayed what he believed in. He was also classified as a spy because he was keeping in contact with his overseas siblings.

He was sent to a jail called the 'Cowshed' by his colleagues at the County Grain Bureau in the city where he worked. His colleagues, who were Communist Party members one day suddenly crashed into Gok's home, looking for evidence that they hoped would prove Gok was an enemy of the Communist Party. As soon as they opened up their imaginations, they would start to look for, or even create things that would prove them right. They only found mine and Kai's letters. Luckily none of the words there could give them what they wanted. They did however find Gok's little notebook in which he wrote down the business done when he worked as a boatman. Gok was hoping one day to pay back the debts he owed to our uncle, who kindly took care of him and Kai. But no one was going to accept his explanation. They took him back to the County Grain Bureau building and locked him in a small room.

'Are you going against Communism?' one of his colleagues shouted at him.

'Are you expecting to get those payments back from poor people? Is that your reason for writing these amounts down? Do you wish to go back to capitalism like the old times?'

'Exploit our workers again? I told you this is a pipe dream. No more,' another colleague shouted at him.

Gok denied it. One of them kicked him behind his back when Gok was forced to kneel on the concrete floor.

Ironically they lived in the same building owned by the Grain Bureau; everyone pretended nothing had happened, including Gok and his wife and son.

Gok had to leave home and workplace, instead working as a pig farmer and he ploughed and sowed rice as a Cowshed prisoner. 'I did very well and quite enjoyed it actually. My pigs grew up much more quickly than the others and my vegetables were grown very green without pig bite marks,' Gok told me. But what he didn't tell me, was that for over two years, he was only allowed back home to his wife and son twice, and had lost almost half his body weight.

Gok never talked about what he had been through and the outcome of his connection to Kai and me who lived overseas. But after all, it didn't stop him from secretly listening to the *Voice of America Chinese* broadcast at night. He had to find out what was going on outside the world where his sister and brother lived. He knew things that most Chinese didn't know.

Before he went to bed, Gok stayed in his little bedroom, put earphones on with the volume as low as he could, then turned on the radio and slowly turned and turned the dials until he found the station. It was dangerous as it could have been cause for him to be jailed, or even executed by the authorities.

I suddenly realised that's why Gok insisted he wanted a good-quality radio for his son. I bought the best brand: the German-made Grundig, a small size, with a black leather case and a long antenna that could be extended. It easily received the signal and heard the broadcast much more clearly. I was glad.

Postscript

Since the China trip, Ella had never stopped talking about it and always wanted to return.

She died in a nursing home alone in her sleep.

'I wish I could die in my sleep, Ella,' I told her when I visited her grave. 'You can go anywhere you like now,' I even joked.

12.2. Humpbacked Qun and Her Blue-Eyed David

Almost everyone knew Qun in Edinburgh. Sometimes people would see a hunchbacked Chinese woman with one arm holding onto a tall and handsome white young man—they would talk and smile like mother and son, shop or have afternoon tea in a nice tea room. They ignored the looks of some passing by. They were Qun and David—the nanny and her master's son.

Qun was a 'self-comb woman' from Guangdong. This meant she was a girl who had decided not to marry. They put up their hair in a bun at the back, like a married woman. They were special individual groups supporting each other. They may buy a house together and live under the same roof for the rest of their lives. They worked mostly as wealthy family's servants, or nannies like Qun.

Originally, Qun and her fellow villagers were planning to go to Singapore to build paved roads. But on the first day in Hong Kong, all her money was stolen. She was forced to stay in Hong Kong alone. After more than three years of working different kinds of hard labour, and then selling souvenirs on Wan Chai Pier, she became a nanny for a wealthy family. That was her dream job, and she was good at it.

'I cooked fish without a fishy smell, fresh and just perfectly meat-off-the-bone,' she often told everyone proudly. That skill was something to be proud of as a Southern Chinese woman. 'My David-boy loved it. He said no one else in the world could cook fish like me.'

'Don't tell me I didn't teach you how to do it, you just can't learn my skills, I have magic hands,' she kept saying. That was so true. At least I couldn't do it.

David was the only son of a high-ranking British naval officer in Hong Kong. When David was still in his mother's womb, twenty-six-year-old Qun was hired, waiting for David to be born.

In 1966, David's father was recalled to Edinburgh by the Scottish government, and Qun followed them to Edinburgh. The reason was simple. Teenaged David told his parents that if Qun stayed in Hong Kong, he would also stay in Hong Kong.

Qun lived on the same street as my China Garden. That one-bedroom on the first floor was rented by David's parents. They paid three years of rent upfront for her.

They also found her a job as a cleaner in a small hotel on the other street behind.

Most afternoons, when she finished her work, just before the China Garden did its lunch, Qun's broad body shape appeared on time at our door.

'Have you eaten yet?' was her everyday greeting.

Then, she would walk down to the kitchen, roll up her sleeves, and wash the dirty dishes if there were any left, even if there was just one. She didn't mind packing up the rest of our staff meals into a big bowl if there was some left, saying it was going to be her late-night snack, or her breakfast when she went to work the next morning. The big bowl would be returned the next day.

She came so routinely, I forgot that before she started, there were always some dirty dishes left in the sink and that the staff meal was always unfinished too.

If one day we didn't see her, the next day she often told us, 'I had tea with my David-boy in Jenner department store,' or, 'David-boy drove me to the fish market.' What she and David had eaten, where they had been, and what he had said, were the topics Qun talked about most.

'Doris, if your daughter isn't too fat, maybe I will ask David-boy to think about her,' Qun said to me on a summer day. 'I don't understand, you are so skinny, but your daughter isn't, what did you feed her?'

A few years later Qun planned to open a restaurant like me. It was David who found an empty shop and did all the planning permissions. Then he bought a dozen old school desks and chairs and altered them into dining tables and chairs.

One day I went to see Qun, and I saw David sawing wood outside the door. Qun grabbed a towel to help him wipe off the sweat.

'Aunty Doris,' David raised his head, a blond-haired, blue-eyed young Scottish man with a warm smile and neat white teeth. His favourite nanny Qun always said they were to her credit because every one of David's teeth was pulled out by her with a small string, right on time, so that the new teeth would not grow crooked.

'Nanny Qun will open on the eighth of next month. As you knew, the eighth is a good day. It means rich and richer.' David often spoke to us in half English and half Cantonese with some of Qun's dialect—very funny.

I asked Qun why David was so nice to her.

'He was born with a good heart. How much could I teach him? But…' Qun said, 'I changed his first nappy, I fed him his first fish congee without hairline fish bones, I taught him his first walk, I carried him and sang to him all night long when he had a fever.'

I have secretly studied David's physiognomy. His nose was round and thick, his eyes were bright and soft, and his forehead was full and lustrous, which matched the description of a 'good man' in the old books. It would be better if the ears were longer—his ears were too small on his head I thought.

Qun's restaurant was called 'Hong Kong Island' and was the same name as the place where David grew up in Hong Kong. It had only nine tables, but it was one of the most prosperous Chinese restaurants in Edinburgh. Many of the guests were well-intentioned. It was not because the food was delicious or the service was particularly good, it was because it was David's nanny's restaurant, and David often waited tables on weekends. He carried the dishes in and out happily. And also because every year, at the most important review ceremony in Edinburgh, David's father was one of those people who was sitting in the front row, without fail, in a military uniform pinned full of medals.

Years after, Qun became one of the richest Chinese in Edinburgh.

In addition to buying her restaurant property, she also bought ten other properties in Edinburgh and turned them into restaurants and takeaway shops. Qun had big rental incomes.

But Qun was still Qun, a frugal person who even had to pack leftover fish bones for her next meal.

Almost half of Qun's entire life in Edinburgh was in that ten-square-metre kitchen. She became more and more bent at the waist. She used to be about the same height as me, but when she was older she was as tall as my shoulders.

Twenty-five years later, she suddenly fell beside the large metal kitchen sink. Hong Kong Island became Qun's final destination.

Qun had no relatives in England or Hong Kong. Only some long-distance relatives in China where she had hardly been back to. Qun knew that because she was a self-comb woman, she was to be treated as a married woman who had left her home. This meant her ashes would not be allowed to be brought back to the village, which Qun was actually very much hoping for, to be with her parents.

She said to us sometimes, 'If I died, I would be like a wild ghost and a lonely soul drifting, no roots.' Then she would say, 'Edinburgh has long been the last destination in my life journey, it has treated me well.'

Thinking of this, I felt relieved for her.

The Hong Kong Island closed not long after Qun's death. None of the Chinese were brave enough to take it over because many people believed that Qun would not leave the kitchen.

It soon became an Indian restaurant.

Three years after Qun's death, David tragically died. That summer, while David was with his wife and three children on a holiday in the Mediterranean Sea, when a big ship passed by, it caused an unexpected powerful wave which smashed David, who was sitting on the side of their boat, into the sea. He was swept underneath the boat.

His wife buried David with his beloved nanny Qun, following his wishes.

The old physiognomy book did say that people with long ears will live longer. Sadly, David had small ears.

12.3. Vietnam Refugees, Mr and Mrs Chee

My car had just stopped outside the China Garden; I saw Mrs Chee was coming, again.

'Boss, you work too hard really, let me help you.' Mrs Chee attentively carried out a heavy whole bag of carrots from my car boot, then a box of green peppers and beansprouts, 'We must be quick, otherwise you will get a ticket fine from that uniformed man I saw on the corner over the road.' Mrs Chee smiled with her two tiger teeth and two dimples.

Mrs Chee's husband was the new kitchen staff I hired the week before. His main job was to wash dirty dishes and then help with whatever needed to be done in the kitchen. He was the most leisurely employee I had ever hired. It seemed he couldn't finish the washing even if it was only a few tables of business. I was worried he wouldn't be able to do the job on weekends.

On Friday afternoon, I found a woman standing by Mr Chee helping him with the dishes when I walked into the kitchen.

'I'm his wife; hope you don't mind, boss,' she said, 'I work in a takeaway shop only a few bus stops from here, I'll come over after work on Fridays and Saturdays, so you don't have to pay me.' Then she came to the upstairs bar and said to me, 'Boss, he has never worked before and doesn't know how to work. I hope you let him stay, please.'

Her request surprised me because I was always the only one who would be worried day and night that the staff would fire me, and I couldn't open my doors.

Mr and Mrs Chee were refugees from Vietnam.

The Chee family were wealthy Chinese living in Saigon who ran a large grocery store business. There were more than twenty Vietnamese and Chinese who worked for them. One of them was a porter who was from a poor village in the mountains.

The daughter of the porter came to Saigon to see her father one day and a smile lit up her round face, as always. The wife of the master of the Chee family liked her tiger teeth and dimples. She thought this girl would be a good wife for her only son, who needed a stronger woman beside him. It didn't take long—she married into the Chees.

A year later she gave birth to a son, then to two daughters. The smart and capable young Mrs Chee also soon learned how to speak Chinese fluently.

In the seventies, the Communist Party of Vietnam confiscated all the property of the Chee family and drove them out of their big house.

'Fortunately, my wife is Vietnamese, so I was not dragged to prison,' Mr Chee told us their story one day when we were having supper after work.

'We knew that Vietnam would not be a place for Chinese to stay anymore. We needed to leave. We tried our best to smuggle out of the country,' Mr Chee said.

Mr Chee paid five gold bars to buy smuggling boat seats for a family of five. There was no chance of being smuggled out of the country without gold bars.

Being intercepted and investigated by members of the Vietnam Communist Party was what they were afraid of most, and they were also scared of being reported by Vietnamese neighbours. That day, they left home separately at different times after dark. Mr Chee and his two daughters pretended to go shopping, and Mrs Chee and son pretended to visit relatives. Everyone however wore several layers of clothing on a hot day and carried no big bags. Everything had to be left behind. They walked crossing the side streets and alleys.

They were told to lie down on the floor quietly in an abandoned farmhouse near the sea with more than fifty people and waited for hours until midnight passed. The smugglers led everyone stumbling onto the boat. The boat quietly left the shoreline to the dark sea.

'It was so dark, like Chinese ink really, not even one star in the sky,' Mrs Chee described. 'No adult could sleep. We were so afraid that anything could have happened.'

The sky was slightly bright, hours later. Someone suddenly saw a Vietnam Communist military ship in the morning fog. People started to scream with panic. The first person to jump into the sea with a wooden life buoy was the owner of the boat. Some people followed. Whether on the boat or in the sea, a frightful muddle.

'We couldn't believe the soldiers opened fire. We were looking for a place to hide—where could we hide?' Mr Chee said. 'I saw my older girl backing away, I quickly pulled her and stuffed her into a pile of ropes with her younger sister.'

'The soldiers boarded the boat and called for everyone to come out.' Mr Chee looked at his wife who was bowing her head and carrying on eating Singapore vermicelli noodles, as if she hadn't heard.

'My younger girl crawled out first with blood on her face. I thought she was shot. But it wasn't her blood, it was her sister's.' Mrs Chee continued the story while shoving noodles into her mouth without looking at other people, she seemed as if she was talking to herself.

The Chee family and others were detained in a temporary detention centre in Saigon. Hundreds of them, all Chinese, had been captured.

Their twelve-year-old daughter lay on a bamboo mat bleeding for two days. No medical treatment was given.

'All her clothes were used to soak up her blood,' Mrs Chee said. 'My girl died without a sound.'

The younger daughter did not cry nor speak until the fourth day when they were released to go home. She said that her elder sister was holding her close to her chest when the bullet slammed into her from the back.

They buried their daughter in the family grave, and began planning how to smuggle out again—there was no other way out, Mr Chee said.

A month later, they handed over eight gold bars; the price had gone up double. The boat was overcrowded with one hundred and twenty-three people, though it could only carry thirty. Sitting on the side of the boat, their feet could dip into the water.

'None of us could swim, except for my son, who was very scared,' Mr Chee said. 'I told my son that if the boat sinks, he has to swim with his sister on his back, and we don't mind feeding the sharks.'

The boat travelled for two days and three nights to the waters of China. A local battered tugboat came and towed their heavy boat out to the open sea as per their arrangement.

Only halfway, the tugboat stopped. They noticed the smugglers were discussing something with the owner of the tugboat in low voices.

The smugglers told them that the tugboat's owner had a son who wasn't that clever, and he was looking for a wife. No concern for appearance, only that she would be young enough to give him children. He warned that if they didn't give them what they wanted, they would loosen the towing and leave them all on the open sea. A few hours later, a young woman called Jen left their boat for the tugboat.

'I knew her. She had a herbal tea shop. Her husband died of illness. She was a widow,' said Mrs Chee. 'She started to cry when people pointed out she was the most suitable woman. A group of people convinced her through coercion and lure. I felt so sorry for her. She was going to meet her brother who arrived in Hong Kong as a refugee early.'

The Chee family lived in a Vietnamese refugee camp in Hong Kong for three years before they were assigned to the UK. They came to Edinburgh because a friend's friend was in Edinburgh. And because their friend heard that I was desperately looking for new kitchen staff, they spent more than one hour walking and asking for directions using the name of my restaurant written down on a piece of paper. They walked straight to the kitchen.

Mrs Chee told my cook that her husband could do the job right away. My cook glanced at him and pointed to the sink in the utility room, 'Over there. The boss went out to buy goods. Ask her about wages when she is back later.' Mr Chee started his job.

When I came back from the market, I saw the mountain of dirty dishes were all clean and tidied. A middle-aged man with glasses was standing beside them with steaming eyes, peeling onions. No one told me that his wife had just left.

On the last Saturday of the China Garden, when the door was about to close, a red-haired girl, wearing heavy makeup, a few different earrings hung on her ears, a lot of rusted jewellery on her wrists and wide-leg jeans, swept all the way from the door to the bar.

'Aunty, I'm here to see my dad.' A breath of smoke.

Seeing her jeans sweeping down the stairs to the kitchen, one of my waitresses whispered to me, 'She has been a few times—every time a different man is waiting outside.' I saw a tall and thin man standing on the street outside the door, smoking a cigarette desperately.

'Bye, bye Aunty,' she smiled, showing two tiger teeth. Besides that, she was a pretty girl.

'Boss, my daughter isn't a mature girl. She didn't have a chance to go to a proper school in Vietnam. Only my husband taught her Chinese at home,' said Mrs Chee who was sitting in my passenger seat as I offered to give them a lift back home that night.

'My daughter is useless,' Mr Chee sighed in the back seat.

On the street after midnight, there were few pedestrians.

'When we came to England four years ago, she was bullied badly in school. Eventually, she told us that if you are tough enough, people will be afraid of you, and that was the only way you could get away from bullying. We are not sure if this is truth or lies, but she is much happier when she comes home from school,' Mrs Chee said.

'My daughter had four or five boyfriends, all of them were *gweilo* boys. We don't mind her dating or marrying a *gweilo*. I hope this boy is serious,' Mrs Chee continued, turning back to look at her husband who was sitting in the backseat and had closed his eyes.

She started to tell me what happened to her daughter among those girls inside the smuggling boat cabin that morning in the sea.

'The soldiers ordered them to take off their tops and pull down their trousers, they used their fingers to dig into every girl's vagina and anus. They said they were looking for gold and silver jewellery, which was probably hidden inside. The youngest was only five years old. No girl dared to tell,' Mrs Chee wiped her eyes and said, 'I was told three years later by my daughter. My husband doesn't know. He should never know about it.'

I felt like a heavy stone was stuck in my chest, my throat was frozen and my hands were shaking. I hoped that Mrs Chee didn't notice my tears. I could not find any words to say to this poor mother.

I was glad that Mr Chee didn't know about his daughter, who had survived bullets and had been brutally and violently sexually attacked by those soldiers when she was only nine years old.

Ten months into my employment of Mr and Mrs Chee, it was the first time I came to their place, and it was one of the worst areas in Edinburgh, where Andrew and his siblings grew up.

No wonder Mr and Mrs Chee wore self-sewn cloth belts around their waists every day, which contained the most valuable things in the family, including photos of their good days in Vietnam.

'Thank you, Boss, thank you,' they nodded and raised their hands many times when I drove away.

12.4. It Was the Final Night of the China Garden

Mr Chee was one of the last staff I hired. I sold my business permits to a young Indian couple. The fourth Chinese restaurant in Edinburgh had ended its journey in 1978. After fifteen years of harsh business, the feeling was mostly: finally, such relief.

My daughter unexpectedly set up mahjong games to celebrate my retirement at home. All my close friends were invited.

'Doris, you got out of all those troubles at last,' Mrs Chan hugged me and said.

Mrs Lee made a cake, it was the biggest she had ever made. 'We aren't going to finish it tonight, are we?' she laughed.

My old staff Ben cooked lobsters with long eggy noodles—it represented good wishes.

Of course, my daughter's aunt, my old friend Pauline, was indispensable. She made taro pancakes which I loved.

They were my lifelong friends; I felt lucky to have them around me when I needed them. We knew each other so well.

That night we laughed, shouted and cheered over the funny bits of our past days.

'Doris, do you remember what I said to you the first time we met in Guangdong House?' the straightforward Mr Chan asked. His wife answered before me: 'Don't give me old overnight fried rice to eat.' It was 1963 when they came to Edinburgh looking for business.

Mrs Chan was well educated. She worked for the bank as a secretary in Hong Kong. She reminded me of Miss Lo who I worked with back in 1943 in Kai Tak Airport—the job with the Japanese that I never mentioned. She fell in love with a famous footballer, Men Chan, who Andrew loved to watch play when we were in Hong Kong. He was a member of the Hong Kong football team that represented China in the 1960s Summer Olympics in Rome.

Then the retired footballer decided to move to the capital of Scotland because his wife thought if the Queen lived in that place it must be a fortunate land.

'Doris, I still owe you teacups, that posh set—you told me they were very expensive,' the loud Mrs Lee said, 'Sorry I keep forgetting.'

'You're never going to buy back Doris the cup set. We have heard that countless times,' Ben muttered.

'This huge cake replaces my posh tea set. You have a deal tonight,' I laughed.

It was a few years before. One night Mrs Lee came to my home to play mahjong. She couldn't wait to show us what kung fu she could do from her class in someone's back garden, who claimed he was once a team member of the Bruce Lee Kung Fu Club in Hong Kong. She shouted and half-squatted down on two legs, her two arms held at her waist with fists ready, then one leg kicked out and one arm transversely waved backwards. She lost balance before we could exclaim, and fell on my coffee table, breaking two sets of cups and saucers. Since then she won a nickname: 'Kung Fu Lee'. We joked about her believing she could do kung fu.

But she proved she really could. One night, near closing time, three men walked into her restaurant. One of the men at the time while enjoying Mrs Lee's husband's large juicy homemade sui mai was talking with his friends around the table. 'Those Chinese eat everything in life, even rats from the fields or insects that have four legs—the worst is the snakes. They are so disgusting, don't you think?'

Mrs Lee was standing behind the bar washing glasses, and heard what this man had said. While her staff looked at each other not knowing how to react, she put down the glasses, went to the table and started to clean while the four men's mouths were still chewing. 'Out! All of you out! No pay!' she said.

'You are a little Chinese rat, go back to where you came from,' the man stood up and shouted with the strong smell of beer.

Mrs Lee threw everything down onto the bar counter and called out, 'Oh *haa!*' She was loud and half-squatted down on two legs, her two arms held at her waist with fists ready.

'They looked shocked, then scrambling, ran to the door,' Mrs Lee laughed her head off when she told us 'Ha, they just didn't know that shouting and that movement is the only kung fu I have learned the most. In fact, I was so scared.'

After using her kung fu to fight back against three men, she even started to claim herself the female Bruce Lee of Edinburgh— taking kung fu to another level. We all made fun of it with her. Her laughter would influence everyone around her, which I liked a lot.

Mrs Lee was a blind-date bride from Hong Kong. She was a nineteen-year-old girl who worked for a small factory sock maker when she first met her husband-to-be, who was fifteen years older. It was 1972. They married after only one month.

'"Marry, marry", that was what my mother kept telling me—isn't a woman just for marrying a man? If not, what for? I'm lucky to be able to marry into England,' Mrs Lee said frankly, 'it was only when I landed in the airport in London and entered a men's toilet that I found out that I don't understand the language of this country. It was too late to regret it, I just had to hold on.'

Years after, Mrs Lee, who despite speaking little English was smart and capable, empowered by the force of money, became the second Qun. She enjoyed buying empty properties around the city, renovating them and licensing them as restaurants and takeaway shops, selling them as leaseholds, and then taking property rent. Her later job was to inspect her shops around town.

That night was truly a most relaxing night that I hadn't had in a long, long time. I almost thought that my life wasn't too bad after winning the mahjong game which my dear friends had intentionally let me win. I just wished Andrew was sitting in his chair watching television. I could hear his laughter sometimes from there, or ask him if he wanted a cup of tea, with warm milk and one spoonful of sugar.

12.5. The Death of Andrew

The trees in Meadows Park were getting taller and taller; no matter if there were good days or bad days, they just kept growing. Leaves fell in yellow and grew back in green, they never missed a season. Wind brushed through the branches, they seemed to dance with happy songs swaying.

'It's a pity, Andrew, they should plant camphor trees in the park. They are easy to grow, and grow big,' I said once to Andrew.

'Yes, darling, they should,' Andrew agreed with a smile, 'I am sure that it is because no one knows that there are better trees in Hong Kong.'

Almost every good day, Andrew walked through those trees to the China Garden to have his lunch, then on to buying a newspaper, *The Scotsman* in the shop next door. He walked home reading it in the afternoon. He was often sitting on that chair I bought for him. He liked to watch his wife carry the meals up and clean the dishes running down to the kitchen while he was eating. He might try to help to clean up the empty glasses on the table sometimes, before he left for home.

One day, a woman rushed into the China Garden and shouted, 'Anyone called Doris here? Her husband has fallen on the street.'

I rushed out.

'We couldn't lift him up, I am so sorry,' the woman started to cry, 'he is too heavy—he said to call his wife Doris.'

Andrew was lying on the street pavement by Meadows Park. He must have tried to step backward when he crossed the road seeing a car coming.

'Darling, I am embarrassed,' Andrew looked up at me, 'I don't think I am hurt, my arms are as strong as always, you know.' He even tried giving me a laugh.

'Roll yourself face down, Andrew, like you do at home,' I said. 'Remember use your elbows to hold your upper body.'

I wiggled myself under Andrew's body and used my back to jack him up. 'Bend your knees now.'

Andrew sat up using his arms and knees slowly.

'My wife, Doris. My wife is stronger than me,' Andrew introduced me with a grin.

The people around us looked dumbfounded at how I could do this to a six-foot-tall and over two-hundred-pound man.

'We have practised at home,' Andrew joked.

Since that fall, Andrew mostly stayed at home, sitting in the living room by the windows and then, was unable to sit up any longer. I moved his bed to the living room to face the windows.

Many times I drove past home and knowing he was alone, waiting for me or Astrid to come home, I couldn't help my tears.

His brother Owen came to visit on some weekends. They talked about their sisters who followed their husbands and moved to the US, and his tough top job in Inland Revenue in Edinburgh.

'Owen has been today,' Andrew said one day. 'Don't worry about your delayed tax payment, he will look at it.'

I paid tax. Yes, there would be a delay, but I have never asked for any money from this country. Except, only once. It was the lower ground floor sisters. Mary and Maggie advised Andrew to apply for illness support from the government, and they even filed the form with him without telling me. One day I received a letter from the government that said we weren't qualified to claim support because I owned a restaurant.

'Andrew, look at what you have done!' I was shouting at Andrew, which I shouldn't have. The shame of it did take me over.

'I am very sorry, darling. Yes, I should know more about these things than you. I just try to help you.' Andrew walked towards me with his trembling body and tried to hug his wife. I sent a cheque back to the tax office with the amount we received, plus the interest I thought right, with a letter that Andrew wrote as an apology.

In eighteen years of Andrew suffering Parkinson's disease, I had witnessed him change from such a strong man, who played football like a tiger, to then become a man unable to hold a pen. I was so sad for him and felt so helpless. But I didn't claim any support from this country.

Christmas of 1977 had never been so dull to me. The bookings for Christmas parties at the China Garden were the lowest since it had opened. Even my house party of mahjong and roast turkey that I hosted every year had to be cancelled.

Mrs Chan insisted on going to the hospital instead of me to keep an eye on Andrew. 'Doris, you must go home, you haven't slept enough these past days,' she said worriedly. 'Don't forget, you have to work tomorrow morning, and you Doris, just had your operation not long ago.'

It was three months before. I didn't notice that I had gastric bleeding. It must have been going on for a while. I was sent to the hospital for emergency surgery. I was exhausted.

'Doris, Andrew has been ill for eighteen years. If not for you, he would have died earlier,' the family doctor said in the hallway. 'It is time to let him stay in the hospital.'

I burst into tears.

On that day, I was trying to feed Andrew congee, sitting on his bed in the ward. It was his favourite, taking two hours to cook with salty pig bones. I blew cool a spoonful of congee, lifting it to Andrew's mouth. Congee dribbled out from the corner of his mouth. I wiped it away and tried again. Tears kept running down my face. And Andrew's.

He had lost the ability to speak and move. Only his eyes stared at me. I knew what he wanted to say: 'Doris, darling, help me—just like you normally do.'

I told him that I really couldn't this time.

'Andrew wasn't good,' Mrs Chan called from the hospital at night, 'the doctor said he could not hold on much longer.'

On a cold snowy night, on December 29th 1977, Andrew passed away at age fifty-seven, without me at his bedside.

'He was sleeping,' Mrs Chan said on the phone. 'Very peaceful.'

I seemed to be paralysed with overwhelming regret that I was so naive to think that Andrew would be better and go home. I couldn't think, and didn't want to move or say anything. I lay in bed without tears. I was grieving from being unable to save him, and that I wasn't even by his side when he passed away. I couldn't stop thinking that if I hadn't gone home that night, I would have been with him at his last moment, then I would have had a chance to tell him that I was grateful that the nineteen-year-old sergeant took me as his wife in Hong Kong, gave me a home and was willing to be that chicken and dog, that I was grateful he forgave me for rarely sitting with him around our dining table, and gave me the power to make most decisions for our life and our family; instead I only could tell him that in front of his grave.

Pauline sat beside my bed almost every day. She held my hands and wept.

Andrew's funeral was well arranged by our twenty-seven-year-old daughter, with her very best friend Carol at her side. She was so helpful, and soon after, she even moved into our home, which was my daughter's request.

Unexpectedly, our goddaughter Lorna sent a larger wreath. Lorna I hadn't spoken to for a few years though she called sometimes. She wrote, 'Rest in peace Godfather. Your goddaughter, Lorna.' At that time she was living with her boyfriend Peter Chow in Hong Kong. The anger towards her divorcing Ivan seemed to begin fading away over time.

13. Lorna, a Flying Phoenix

13.1. Meeting Hong Kong's Governor

It was a special honour, to be beside the former Governor of Hong Kong David Clive Wilson and his lovely wife, Natasha Helen Mary. In 1998, The National Museum of Scotland invited me to its opening ceremony. I don't know how they found me and sent an invitation. It made me realise how extraordinary English detectives were.

Fifty years later, who knew that the first Chinese restaurant in Edinburgh would be knocked down, and now become part of the National Museum of Scotland.

Mr and Mrs Wilson I had met before in Hong Kong at a party I went to with my goddaughter Lorna. Of course, they wouldn't recognise me. I was just a woman who accompanied the wife of Peter Chow, the Secretary for Administrative Service and Information and the Secretary for Home Affairs of colonial Hong Kong at that time.

On that important day to me, I wore my best silk *cheongsam* dress which was beautifully made, solid black satin with gold flowers. Again, the smell of camphor emanated lightly like fresh wind from the forest.

Mr and Mrs Wilson were smiling, 'How are you?' Mr Wilson spoke to me in Cantonese perfectly.

'I'm very good. Thank you,' I replied.

I didn't think Mr Wilson wanted to be the Hong Kong Governor had Sir Edward Young not died in Beijing on December 5th 1986. Mr Wilson replaced him to become the twenty-seventh man in charge of Hong Kong ten years before the handover of Hong Kong to China.

First, he had to change his Mandarin Chinese name from 'Wei Dewei' to 'Wai Yik-Shun' when he became the Hong Kong Governor. This was because the Hong Kong people didn't like the Mandarin pronunciation of his old name. They said that his name in Cantonese sounded too much like 'hypocrisy', and that the surname and the third character can each be divided into components meaning 'one thousand eight hundred female ghosts'. It made his name more like: "double ghosts knocking at the door". But they liked his new name in meaning and sound: 'guard the credibility and the integrity'.

Wilson had been exposed to the importance of a name in Chinese culture. The Chinese believe a bad name will bring bad luck all your life long. Even my goddaughter Lorna always said that the worst thing isn't your destiny, but whether you have been given a bad name.

'He was more like a scholar and an expert on China than a politician,' Lorna said, 'he is too soft for China. He will be removed as the Governor of Hong Kong soon.'

As Lorna predicted, Wilson was succeeded by the politician Chris Patten. He left Hong Kong for his town in Scotland in the summer of 1992. Before he left Hong Kong, he gave fifty thousand British passports to the people who worked for the Hong Kong government as senior officers and their family members, and to those who had contributed to Hong Kong. Lorna had a passport of this kind. She named herself Elisabeth, after the Queen.

'Elisabeth must be a good name—can't go wrong,' Lorna laughed. She used it only for UK entry.

When I told her I met Wilson over the phone, Lorna asked: 'Godmother, why didn't you say hello to Mr Wilson for me? He was so kind to me.'

When Lorna was heartbroken and humiliated by her second husband, Peter Chow, who was Mr Wilson's highest-ranking Chinese officer in the Hong Kong government in the nineties, Mr Wilson chose Lorna's side.

'Mr Wilson called Peter into his office, and advised him not to leave me, that I am a good woman,' Lorna told me. At that time Peter Chow was promoted as the primary ethnic Chinese individual in a secondary-level position in the Hong Kong Government.

13.2. Lorna, a Sparrow and Phoenix

> *Women born under the sign of Libra are very smart, have good interpersonal relationships, are highly capable, pay attention to friends and family, are generous to them, and are very cautious about themselves.*
>
> *The Year of the Rooster woman is witty, humble and brave.*

Lorna is a 'Rooster' woman with the Libra zodiac sign. The most famous Hong Kong fortune teller approved three words in her fortune-telling letter: 'the flying phoenix', and added another four words: 'flying higher and higher'.

In the Qing Dynasty, a seven-character ancient poem describes the life story of a lucky girl Miss Chen: '*The old nest is a swallow of mud, flying on the branches and turning into a phoenix.*' Her story, circulated among people, continues to echo down the centuries. Miss Chen used to make a living by dancing and playing the lute. One day luckily, she was beloved and made prosperous by the king. Just like a little sparrow becoming a beautiful and noble phoenix, standing on the top of the tree.

Certainly, my goddaughter Lorna was one of the many Miss Chens. Lorna has never worked—except for becoming a 'Mrs', and another 'Mrs'. Life—whatever will be, will be. If it's not to be, it's meant not to be, don't push it.

Mrs Lorna Collaco

My neighbours in Diamond Hill, Kowloon, were an educated couple, Mr and Mrs Collaco. They both worked for the bank. Their older son Ivan was quiet and polite.

Every Sunday, Collaco's family of four dressed well and drove to St. Teresa's Church in Waterloo. Sometimes we went as well. Mrs Collaco became my three-month-old Astrid's godmother on the day of her Catholic baptism.

One day their housekeeper Mrs Chen brought her seventeen-year-old daughter Feng to the host's house because Mrs Chen stepped off on the wrong foot when she got off the bus and sprained her ankle. It was Feng who insisted on coming with her mother to help her.

Feng worked in a towel-making factory, where she packed towels since she was fourteen. Her full name was Feng Hao, which meant 'good phoenix', a very popular, good girl's name that her father gave to his youngest daughter.

Twenty-six-year-old Ivan couldn't help but fall madly in love with Mrs Chen's daughter, and told his mother flatly that he must marry this girl.

'She has no education and is not that pretty,' Mrs Collaco said in my house. 'What do you think? Doris?'

'The girl is very smart and sanguine. She could help Ivan a lot,' I said.

'They are very different people, that makes me worry,' Mrs Collaco said, sipping tea and shaking her head. As a senior bank secretary, Mrs Collaco certainly saw more than me.

'I can't stop them, can I?' she said finally, 'but, she must convert to Catholicism.'

Consequently, Andrew and I become Feng Hao's godparents. She was given the foreign name 'Lorna' by Ivan's mother. We signed for her on the church papers and we also had Chinese traditional rites, which Lorna's mother Mrs Chen asked for. We gave Lorna a golden rice bowl and a pair of ivory chopsticks, which meant she would have our blessings for food and drink; and a set of clothes with a red hair ribbon, which meant she was never to be without clothes to wear and for good health. In return, we received two pairs of trousers from Mr and Mrs Chen which symbolised that their daughter's godparents would be wealthy for a long enough time to look after her daughter.

Dainty and petite Lorna bowed down upon her knees three times, then held a cup of Chinese tea, 'Godmother, Godfather, please drink my tea.'

Eighteen-year-old Mrs Lorna Collaco became the youngest member of the Collaco family, upper-middle class in Hong Kong.

She lived in a three-bedroom house with a small public garden at the back. No more slums, where those houses built of wood and metal sheets had rats staring by your bedside at night.

She didn't need to get up early and pack a rice bowl into a tin for lunch in the towel maker factory anymore. Her job now was being Mrs Collaco, who did nothing for a living but church jobs for example, helping the poor, and visiting the elderly or disabled people.

There was also no more rush to push and squeeze onto the bus; Lorna now had a little sports car and she started to learn English and had a private teacher from church arranged by her mother-in-law.

Ivan was promoted to a high-ranking position in the Hong Kong Immigration Department. With his smart uniform, a sword inside the leather sheathed, he looked very handsome and confident. Pauline could come to England from Hong Kong easily and was quick to obtain an entry visa because of my goddaughter's husband.

Lorna and Ivan had moved to the Senior Civil Servant Dormitory in West Central after three years of marriage. Their neighbourhood was composed of families who were enjoying the privileges of being part of Hong Kong's Disciplined Service. The wives brought a lot of jolly and gossip around the neighbourhood too.

On the third floor, one of the apartments was resided by a senior officer, Peter Chow who worked in the Health

Department, where once my dear old friend Mr Dr Selwyn-Clarke was the first person in charge from 1933-43.

Rumours were going around that Mr Chow's wife was having an affair with an English lawyer. Their three young children were always left at home with their father.

Lorna met him for the first time when she joined the netball club. Mr Chow was holding his youngest daughter by her arm and was followed by his two older sons walking down the stairs. He radiated an infectious enthusiasm with a manly charm that attracted Lorna deeply.

'Your children are so cute,' Lorna said.

At the time, she and Ivan were still waiting for their child to come. They wanted to start a family, but sadly had no signs of it. Then housewife Lorna began to love being Peter's babysitter, for free.

People started to hear love songs more often; the versatile Peter sat on his balcony and played his guitar passionately. New gossip passed around, like that those songs he was singing was for one of the apartments on the first floor.

'I knew that this was going to happen,' Mrs Collaco wrote. 'Ivan should let her go, it is the only way. She isn't the right girl for my son, just like I said.' Mrs Collaco never liked her daughter-in-law, Lorna knew it.

Thirteen years after their tumbledown marriage, Ivan had let go of Lorna's hands. I didn't think he had a choice because everyone knew that Peter Chow was getting a divorce from his wife and leaving his children to live with Lorna.

Heartbroken and humble Ivan would let Lorna go if Peter swore to him that he would never leave Lorna, and to promise him that he would look after Lorna for the rest of her life.

In a long letter from the old Mrs Collaco, she told me her son suffered great pain and humiliation from Lorna. I stopped talking to Lorna till after Andrew's funeral.

Mrs Lorna Chow

Lorna and Peter flew to Edinburgh for the first time together just after Andrew's funeral. It was very nice to see them, to be honest.

Lorna was a new Lorna—except for her laughter. She looked mature and dignified in a beige tweed skirt suit and black heeled shoes. There was no doubt that Peter was a vigorous and energetic man to which Ivan couldn't be compared. No wonder Lorna was attracted.

That weekend, Peter insisted on waiting at the China Garden to help. 'Godmother, I have three pounds in tips,' Peter was so happy when he was given tips. 'Godmother, a customer complimented my English was quite correct, and my service was outstanding. I am thinking of what I should buy with these three pounds.' That night I received a bunch of red roses from him.

In 1983 one morning, after more than three years as a girlfriend living in the same house, Lorna was called by Peter: 'Bring your identification card with you, I am sending the driver to pick you up for lunch.' He had just been promoted from director of the Trade and Industry Department to the director of the Hong Kong Information Service Department. Peter Chow was in high and vigorous spirits.

A shiny luxury black car pulled up outside of Hong Kong City Hall, which was built in 1869. Peter was standing by the main door with his suit.

'We are going to marry,' Peter smiled.

He walked forward and embraced Lorna, who stepped out of the car questioningly. Peter kissed her softly, and stroked her curly short hair. As Peter had promised at the beginning eight years ago, he would make Lorna Mrs Chow.

Lorna signed her name on the marriage certificate in tears. She was finally no longer just that woman who only lived with Peter Chow; now she was 'Mrs Chow', formally. The next day, the news was all over the newspapers in Hong Kong.

'I was shocked, Godmother, I had no preparation,' Lorna sounded overwhelmed. 'Thankfully, I was wearing one of my best suits in cream.' Lorna felt that her future had been secured.

When Peter was posted to Brussels as a representative for Hong Kong's trade relations with the European Union, I was invited to their home in Geneva. I stayed with them for three months. It was the best holiday of my life.

On a quiet morning, Lorna and I were sitting on the large patio having breakfast. Lake Geneva was just beside us, beautifully peaceful, like a fairytale with stunning scenery and romance all around.

Lorna said, 'Godmother, I must pinch myself sometimes. How can I live in the most beautiful place on the planet, driving a sports car in Europe with a CC diplomatic plate?' She paused and took a deep breath, 'I knew you thought I was selfish for leaving Ivan. I feel very guilty and sorry too,' her voice choked. 'I was young and naive. Ivan as you know is a quiet person, with no interest or passion. We were two different people who got married by mistake.'

'It's been years, and Ivan is also married. I don't always blame you. As long as Peter is good to you,' I consoled her.

'Ivan's new wife was my friend; I introduced her to Ivan, and hoped they could become a couple. She is more suitable for Ivan than me. I couldn't leave Peter anymore, Godmother, do you understand?' Lorna said with a tone of begging for forgiveness.

Seeing Peter walking out of the kitchen, he went straight behind Lora, put his arms around her, and bent over, kissing her lips gently. They looked very much in love. I felt happy for Lorna.

The men came from all over the world. One day, they had enough of the trade quota negotiations. It was stressful negotiating for everyone, I guessed.

'We must invite them for dinner. Lorna, you and Godmother can do it tonight,' Peter suggested when he came home. 'We have secured an excellent deal for Hong Kong today.' He was always smart enough to do so, I have to say.

The order came, and I was the head chef of the house.

That day, I created some new dishes that Peter gave names to that we had never heard before. 'Ants on Trees' was sesame seeds over mixed vegetables; 'Gui Fer Chicken' was cooked with mixed soy sauce, and the one they liked the most was the 'Lion's Head Ribs' which involved cooking with sugar and malt vinegar, then adding some Worcester sauce. That evening, by the beautiful lake in Geneva, the ten important businessmen were peacefully enjoying the meal I created with Lorna.

Peter kissed me good night and joked, 'Godmother, you should open another restaurant—you must put them on your menu, I guarantee it will bring you good business.' I knew he didn't really mean it, he was just being nice to me.

Peter's excellent job in Brussels brought him back to Hong Kong. He was promoted to a much higher position by Governor Sir Edward Young. As the Secretary for Administrative Services and Information and also the Secretary for Home Affairs; he became the top Chinese man in the Hong Kong Government's office. He had a direct line to the Governor via a phone on his bedside table. People in Hong Kong referred to him as the 'Number Four Chair'—even his car number was number four.

Lorna and Peter were given a house to live in as their home on the Peak. The four-bedroom house had the best view of the Hong Kong skyline. Standing outside on the large terrace, Hong Kong was under your feet. The beauty of the skyline at night was breathtaking.

When I visited Hong Kong, I mostly stayed in their home instead of in my brother Kai's little council flat. Their house was decorated elegantly. Every single piece of furniture in the rooms and every painting on the walls was selected by Lorna. In the living room, the most significant things were the big photos of Lorna and Peter smiling; they were hanging on the wall above the large cream sofa. They looked happy, smart, and posh.

When I arrived at Hong Kong airport for the first time as Peter's wife's godmother, he was holding a bunch of flowers waiting at the special exit. He called me Godmother and hugged me in front of his retinue, which included the high-ranking officers of Hong Kong Customs. Peter's driver opened the door for him, he opened the door for me. I was invited by him to Hong Kong to join his CBE ceremony in 1989; I was there instead of his mother.

Of course, their home was surrounded by security guards and serviced by two housekeepers. Wherever Lorna and I wanted to go, the car with the 004 number plate was waiting. A rule for the drivers was that they were only to talk when asked to. I played mahjong with well-known people in Hong Kong. I entered mainland Guangzhou through a special channel from Hong Kong and Chinese customs because Mrs Chow was with me. I gained a lot of advantages from Lorna.

The eighties was the best time to start my retirement. China's opening up and reform began its 'honeymoon' with the West. My brother's political designation went from a traitor to a hero of the Chinese government. Because he was a member of the East River Column, this history made him one of the most respected people thanks to a new rule for retired veteran cadres or groups which recognised their experience as a unique qualification under the new leadership and rules. His past as a Chiang Kai-shek soldier, his little notebook, and his overseas siblings seemed not to bother them anymore. He was treated very well. His retirement pension was higher than other retirees. His medical treatments were free until his death. He was also given a three-bedroom apartment.

Once he came to Hong Kong to meet me and Kai. Lorna invited them for dinner. In the evening, Gok sat with Peter on the terrace. A communist, and opposite him, a senior British colonial official serving the Queen, talked for quite a while with green tea and Hennessy X.O brandy on the table. Afterwards, Peter said to me in the kitchen, 'Godmother, Uncle is completely brainwashed by communism.'

Lorna added, 'Let him be—that will keep him safe in China.' She was smart.

Though I never could understand why being kept out of the Communist Party, which he had done everything to try and join, became the biggest regret of Gok's life.

Gok's wife said to me once, 'Your brother wouldn't have married me if it wasn't for him just wanting to start a family, because he thought I was a big landlord's daughter, who must hate the Communist Party that executed her father. He and I are not the same kind of people. He is a complete adherent to the Communist Party.' It was then I understood why Gok and his wife slept in separate beds, then in separate rooms later. I don't think Gok had a happy marriage; it was mostly for this reason.

When Lorna became lawfully Mrs Chow, she turned into one of the most powerful 'Mrs' in Hong Kong. She was inevitably involved in Peter's job. People who had already earned enough money and now wanted honorary status would try their best to get to know Lorna. They would hope that she would go home and persuade her husband to recommend them to the Governor because they hoped they could be nominated to be a chair, like Justice of the Peace or even like Chairman of the Tung Wah Group of Hospitals. They wanted the honorary title.

Some businessmen hoped to hear from Lorna about the Hong Kong Government's auction of land prices. Even a little wind, leaking from the gaps of Chow's teeth could make some people very rich. Some super property developer who regretted winning the land auction begged Lorna to go home and talk to Peter, citing the government's disagreement with the price to get his company out of the deal.

'This man can't be trusted, no matter how rich nor how good-looking he is,' Lorna summarised.

At one dinner event, a casino tycoon sent Lorna a gift. His secretary handed a well-wrapped bag to her and said, 'My boss heard that your birthday is coming up next week. If you could accept his small gift, he will be very pleased.'

It was a beautiful ruby ring with diamonds around it, sitting on a blue velvet box. Lorna called the secretary the next day and invited him and his boss for lunch. The ring was returned in its original wrapping.

'It was a waste of my time really, and I ate an expensive lunch that didn't fill me up. I planned to go to a street food stall with Peter for wanton noodle soup,' Lorna said with a smile. Lorna freely admitted that they were in the poorest top ranks of the Hong Kong government.

The Sino-British negotiations in the 1980s were in full swing. Some people instructed Lorna to arrange a dinner party so they could set up a trap for a Chinese government official. Lorna flatly refused.

'Although I don't read much, and have a lower education; I still know what to do and what not to do, what is right and what is wrong—and who is a real friend.' This was what she said quite often.

I believed that even after all those years passed by, Lorna was still welcome in Hong Kong high society because she wasn't arrogant and wasn't greedy. Importantly, she had her own opinions which she thought reflected integrity.

As Peter's position rose higher, his arrogance grew more. No one could deny his ability to get the job done, but at the same time, no one disagreed with his ego and arrogance, as well as his sharp insights. He was famously nicknamed 'Bad Boy Chow' in the headlines.

He once threw a newspaper at Sir Donald Tsang's face and shouted at him, 'You are stupid and an idiot!' This 'stupid' person later became the second Chief Executive of Hong Kong. Hard to imagine that the future second chief executive was also standing by his desk, humiliated by his boss at the time.

Peter was also very vocal with his opinions in newspapers and in television interviews about who could be the first chief executive after 1997, when China took over Hong Kong. He was refused his entry application by the Chinese government, even though he was the private information director for the governor of Hong Kong at that time. 'None of you who want this position have the ability to be the Chief Executive, except Tung Chee-hwa.' He said in an interview.

Sharp and charming Peter was right, no matter how much people disliked him. Tung Chee-hwa became the first Chief Executive. Sir Donald Tsang was eventually sent to prison for corruption.

Then Mrs Lorna Chow was always the one who cleaned up his mess with the people around him. It wasn't just Sir Donald Tsang, it could be his driver or his house servants; she hoped to reduce their hatred as much as possible.

Apart from that, Mrs Chow had other jobs to do, including playing mahjong with those wives and girlfriends, listening to what their thoughts were about everything going on in Hong Kong, and then going home to advise her husband. Sometimes she even edited her husband's speeches because she knew what people liked and what people disliked.

'Why did you say that about his company in your speech; his wife told me that her husband won't like it,' Lorna would advise her husband at home.

When Lorna had to host dinners for those people, they came with huge expectations at the dinner table. My clever goddaughter spoke with those important Western guests cheerfully and humorously in English. Nobody noticed that this well-dressed and decent lady had only been to school for a few years formally. She learned everything through her charm.

At a charity event, Lorna jumped into a swimming pool on a chilly autumn day with her cocktail dress on, because the famous singer Leslie Cheung said, 'Lorna if you jump in, I will donate a hundred thousand Hong Kong dollars.' She just put down her drink, kicked off her high heels, and in exclamation, jumped into the pool.

When I quickly handed over a large towel to her, another singer, her good friend Danny Chan, pulled it on her and chased after Leslie to write that big cheque. Sadly both singers committed suicide one after the other. It shocked the Chinese all over the world, not just Hong Kong. Lorna still talked about that charity event years after with laughter and tears.

It wasn't a surprise that in Peter's autobiography, he did not deny that Lorna was the most helpful woman to him during his career with the Hong Kong Government. She had become a woman far away from that eighteen-year-old towel factory girl. She was a phoenix standing on a branch and singing nobly, surrounded by people. What the fortune teller said about her was so right, I realised. But, the phoenix standing on the tree would fall one day if there was a gust of wind. What if another swallow was wanting to become a phoenix? I couldn't stop thinking about it. So was Lorna herself.

She knew that her 'lady-killer' boyfriend and husband Peter Chow had a few girlfriends, including secretaries, first-class airline waitresses, and colleagues.

'They were just my emotional sustenance, or just sex; they came to me—would I be that stupid to refuse?' Peter had his good reasons, always.

'What can I do, Godmother?' Once, she flew over to Edinburgh after a blazing row over her husband checking into a hotel with an air hostess. 'He does it again and again; never thinks of the hurt he causes me,' she cried.

Apart from comforting her, I didn't have enough good reasons nor courage to persuade her to leave this marriage. In her middle age, Lorna, who hadn't worked for most of her life—how could she survive? If she had children perhaps, but she hadn't. I said to her: 'Do you want to stay in Edinburgh, open a takeaway shop, and earn some money spending the rest of your life here? Most importantly, he still comes home to you every day and pays your expenses—you are still his wife, others are not.' I seemed to be taking it easy, but I was very worried and sad. How helplessly hopeful for a woman I knew that knew better. Lorna flew home and carried on being Mrs Chow.

Eventually in a weekend edition of the Hong Kong newspaper Astrid bought from the Chinese supermarket, I saw a photo of Peter with a young woman walking into a five-star hotel. She was young, tall, with long hair. She wasn't Lorna. But there was a small photo of her, inset at the corner.

'Wow, again. Look at this man, 'Astrid reading it said loudly, 'No man is good in this world, as I always thought—really.' My daughter had left the secretary job since she returned home from travelling from Canada, where her best friend Carol's mother lives. Now she was a waitress, working with Carol who was a chef assistant in the same restaurant. They never liked Lorna.

'I knew one day this would come. Sooner or later, isn't it?' Carol added with a sneer, 'A Thai girl? She won't let go as long as she's hooked onto him. Let's see,' Carol took a closer look, 'she must be thirty years younger than Lorna, and she looks much prettier too.'

'Mother, are you going to call Lorna? See what she is going to do about it. Don't tell me she is going to swallow it again this time.'

'I don't think she will divorce Peter.' Carol seemed sure, 'she quite enjoys being Mrs Chow even with so much gossip going on. Yes, how could she throw that away?'

'I think that she will feel the same pain as Ivan. He loved her so much and she knew it. Now it's her turn. What a consequence.'

'Maybe she's crying now,' Carol said, 'I told you, good men are all dead in this world.' She looked at Astrid.

'Why don't you call her now, Mother?' Astrid handed over the international telephone call card.

'She is a fifty-year-old big girl. She knows what she should do,' I said. I knew full well they didn't care about her; mostly, I felt that they were quite happy to see this happen to Lorna, who they didn't like and were jealous of because she was always being praised by me, and was looked up to by all my friends in Edinburgh. Astrid couldn't bear the bad feeling of Lorna bringing that joy to me that she couldn't. 'Yes, she can give you things I can't, I am a useless daughter, Mother,' Astrid said often.

Carol hid her dislike of Lorna very well, specifically in front of Lorna or my friends. Just like how she hid her dislike of me in front of them.

'Lorna couldn't survive without a man. Except for luck, she has nothing really.' Carol must have said this every time Lorna was brought up in conversation. 'God is always fair, that is why she had no children, her children were always someone else's—isn't that true?'

Carol was very convincing to Astrid, who nodded her head a few times.

Peter did offer to let Lorna carry on as Mrs Chow, but: she must keep one eye open and keep one eye shut on his relationship with this Thai girl.

'If you are not divorced from me, you can share my pension and you will receive my pension for the rest of your life if I die. What can you do if you leave me?' I guessed that Peter puffed smoke from his cigar towards the ceiling and said to a crying Lorna. 'What I am doing is just for your own good.'

'I will send her back to Thailand. I will only visit her once every two weeks.' Peter saw that Lorna didn't say a word and said, 'I am still your husband, and will come home after work.'

Heartbroken and helpless Lorna nodded her head. She even said to him that she would give him two years with his lover. The door will keep opening for him. I can imagine that Peter must have let out a long sigh of relief in the cigar smoke, looking across the table at Lorna weeping.

Soon there were more photos of Peter with his girlfriend Miss Soon in the newspapers, even if they were in Thailand. A few days visiting Thailand became months of staying in Thailand. Miss Soon came to Hong Kong too; they lived together in the Hong Kong Regent Hotel. Soon, young and beautiful Miss Soon got a lovely apartment in Bangkok bought for her by Peter.

Mr Peter Chow had forgotten he had a wife at home. He seemed very comfortable with what he was doing, humiliating and hurting her. People began to criticise the behaviour of the Secretary for Home Affairs of Colonial Hong Kong. Even Mr Wilson.

'My wife has accepted it. If she can forgive me, why can't the others?' the arrogant bad boy Peter said to the journalists in an interview. The last of Lorna's dignity had been destroyed by Peter in front of millions.

She called her good friend, Mr Lo Tak-Shing, a lawyer. Mr Lo was a well-known, well-respected person whose registered car plate was number eighteen—one of the twenty numbered car licence plates that the British Government in Hong Kong had issued to senior officers since 1908.

Divorce started. Anger instead of tears for Lorna. To save himself, Peter wrote a big cheque and gave a last try to buy back his wife's petition for divorce. Lorna cashed the cheque and left the petition in court. She insisted that the payment was for being his girlfriend and wife and a work partner for nearly fifteen years. I more than agreed with her. It was a one million Hong Kong dollar cheque.

The last time Lorna and I sat on the terrace of her home was in the early summer of 1991 in Hong Kong. Everything remained—the security guards, the housekeepers, the driver with the number 004 car, but no Peter. Under our feet, the breathtaking Victoria Harbour skyline looked much more stunning than before.

Lorna asked to come to Edinburgh to be with me for a while. I answered, not Edinburgh, but go to London. I will never forget that look on Lorna's face, beyond disappointment, holding back tears that almost rushed out. I didn't tell her that her seventy-three-year-old godmother wasn't a master in her own home anymore, and that Astrid and Carol wouldn't welcome her. They would give her as hard a time as they gave me.

In despair, Lorna left Hong Kong for Taiwan and studied Mandarin at University, arranged for her by her old friend Anna Chennault, the wife of Claire Lee Chennault, a Major General of the Flying Tigers. It was purely to escape from the humiliation and pain. I felt self-accused and was full of remorse for many years that I didn't reach out my hands to Lorna when she fell from the tree, back to a sparrow.

Soon after, Peter Chow was asked to step down from his position before he retired. More precisely, he was abandoned by the government. One of the reasons was for saying: 'Yes, I will emigrate after 1997' on morning television on the *News at Six* in front of millions of Hong Kong people who were worried about their future when 1997 arrived. I was quite sure that if he was still with sophisticated Lorna, he wouldn't have said that so stupidly.

Later, Peter was offered a job at TVB, the biggest television station in Hong Kong. When I saw him dress like an old-style Chinese woman on an entertainment programme, I felt very embarrassed, as did Lorna.

'I have no eyes to see him on these cheap television shows,' she said on the phone.

Astrid and Carol were laughing hysterically, 'Look, Lorna's Peter, look!'

The water that bears the boat is the same that swallows it up—never forget that saying. Women are made of water. This is old Chinese thought.

Peter called once and invited me to his Thailand home. He still called me Godmother. I appreciated he was being kind to me, but of course, I didn't go, because Lorna had said: 'He abandoned your goddaughter—me—and I have been humiliated; slapped in the face by this arrogant man—I hate him.'

Peter died of a heart attack in Thailand at his home in 2005 at the age of seventy-two. I thought if he still had Lorna as his wife, he would have lived longer, because Lorna took good care of him; of what he ate.

Mrs Lorna Wang

The fortune teller had also written on Lorna's fortune-telling paper: 'There is no child; but someone else's children.'

When Lorna was Mrs Collaco, the eighteen-year-old wasn't that keen on having children. When she became Mrs Chow, she was very much looking forward to becoming a mother. One summer she came to Edinburgh from Hong Kong to meet the top obstetrics and gynaecology specialists at the Royal Infirmary. That summer, all my friends in Edinburgh were looking forward to Lorna arriving because she brought things that ordinary people couldn't: fifty braised pigeons, a large box of fresh Thai mangoes, a few famous Jinhua hams, and even a large box of durian meat. These were the things her godmother loved to eat. She was full of hope that world-leading medical technology could give her children. She was only thirty-six at that time.

Unexpectedly, the obstetrician told Lorna that her uterus was underdeveloped and she couldn't conceive. Peter Chow flew over to Edinburgh when the diagnosis was given to a devastated Lorna. I saw them cuddling, kissing; more kisses, and even more kisses—just like a man and woman madly in love.

'My children are your children,' Peter comforted his wife, 'you have been looking after them since they were little. 'After being the mother of Peter's children the first time, Lorna became someone else's mother a second time.

The second time was to Dr Wang's two adult sons, whose mother had died of cancer two years before. She was the closest friend of the wife of the future chief executive, Mr Tung.

Handsome Dr Wang was an anaesthetist, who was educated in Germany and then owned a clinic in Honolulu. He was tall and mighty; a gentleman who liked to read Chinese poetry, loved Xu Beihong's horse paintings, and appreciated calligraphy. The most important thing was that he fell in love with Lorna when they were first introduced by Mrs Tung in Hong Kong. Lorna re-married three months before Peter did. She became Mrs Wang in 1995.

As her godmother, at Lorna's beautiful wedding reception in the Regent Hotel Hong Kong, I met a lot of people I had seen before and people I hadn't. Unsurprisingly, this included the famous people in Hong Kong. Even though Lorna wasn't Mrs Chow anymore, she never left the upper circle of Hong Kong.

Her mahjong friends that I had played with still were all wives of either high-ranking officers, or super-wealthy men, or well-known writers. One billionaire friend paid for wedding flowers to adorn the Regent Hotel's long staircase secretly; another one of her most powerful friends invited her new family members for dinner at their huge villa at the Peak to show Hong Kong's support to protect her from being looked down on in Hawaii, just in case.

Lorna moved to Honolulu. She lived in a villa overlooking the Pacific. The sunset from her villa home's large balcony was truly as breathtakingly beautiful as the Victoria Peak skyline in Hong Kong.

'I've never been so long respected and taken care of,' Lorna said when she visited me in Edinburgh with her newly wedded husband. 'His knowledge of civil culture is unparalleled among my men. Godmother, I'm so lucky to have him at the halfway point of my life.'

Lorna, now Mrs Wang, began a peaceful and completely different life in a foreign country. There were no servants, no drivers, and no friends. She gradually became a veritable housewife who came to Edinburgh by economy class and brought me lint-free easy-to-use rags, Vietnamese prawn cakes, and foldable supermarket shopping bags.

The good things were that her face was radiant, her hair was still curly and graceful, her nails were varnished a beautiful and trendy colour, and she still wore an expensive brown fur jacket.

After just three years of marriage, Lorna's husband was diagnosed with prostate cancer. For the next fifteen years, Lorna became her husband's home nurse. She said to me with a wry smile, 'God is fair: how much you got then is how much you will pay back.'

Dr Wang left a substantial amount of money to Lorna when he passed away. This good man made sure she kept the lifestyle she was used to.

In his last moments, Dr Wang grabbed Lorna's hand close to his chest and murmured, 'Lorna Wang is my wife, Lorna Wang is my wife, my wife.'

'His last words made me feel how much weight I had in his heart, and everything I did was worth it,' Lorna said sobbing.

The simple words 'my wife' for Lorna were especially affectionate. I thought it was because she had never felt herself the wife of her first husband Ivan, because she was still a teenager who didn't understand fully what it meant to be a wife.

She had never felt herself a wife to her second husband Peter Chow too, because she was never treated as one. But she felt she was the wife of her third husband, because Dr Wang called her 'my wife' a few times in his last moments.

Lorna fell for three men in her life. Peter Chow was the man who held Lorna up to stand on a crumbling branch as a phoenix. He was never her favourite. Lorna's favourite was Dr Wang. And, she was Ivan's favourite.

Once, when she was in Edinburgh, she asked me for Ivan's telephone number. Ivan had moved to London with his wife and two daughters before the 1997 Hong Kong handover to China. Lorna insisted that she must say sorry to him this time. When she called out his name over the phone, there was no answer on the other side. Lorna knew he was there. She told him. It took a while to hear Ivan put down the phone. Six years later, Ivan died.

Lorna moved back to Hong Kong from Honolulu. She rented an apartment in a decent area, and with her later husband's money, she continued her daily life: mostly playing mahjong with those people well known in Hong Kong—not much different from being Mrs Chow.

And I, her godmother, started my later life with my daughter and her best friend Carol.

14. Astrid, Carol and Jane

My mahjong friends started to be less and less in number as I got older and older. Astrid drove my mahjong friends away by walking into the living room with abomination written all over her face, and even closed the door with an undignified slam behind her. It seemed she disliked playing; she just wanted to show who was in charge inside this house now. Especially when Mrs Chan's husband died while we were too busy playing.

That night he was leaving my home early when his wife reminded him, 'Don't forget to close the front gate.' He waved at her without looking back.

After eight rounds of mahjong, it was already three o'clock in the morning. Mrs Chan's car pulled into their driveway and she found that her husband's car wasn't there, and no lights were on in the house. She went back to my house and found her husband's silver Mercedes-Benz still on the side of the street. His frozen body was lying on the ground beside the car door. He died of a heart attack.

'If I didn't play mahjong, I would have gone home with him, I would have called an ambulance in time, and he wouldn't have died.' Mrs Chan blamed herself, as did I. She never touched mahjong again. Astrid placed my half-century-old mahjong tiles on top of the tall kitchen unit cabinet with a good reason; she also removed the four legs from the mahjong table and left them behind the long heavy wooden cabinet at the bottom of the stairs.

'Mother, I will take it out when you are going to play,' she said. I remember they were only taken out when my goddaughter Mrs Lorna Wang came to visit because Lorna insisted, and Astrid was afraid of Lorna finding out her mother hadn't played mahjong for ages.

But luckily I found happiness in a Chinese senior lunch club. I could escape from home for half a day. Tuesday was the day I looked forward to. I met new friends and had a simple lunch; the grilled snapper with garlic was my favourite. Most people there called me Aunty Doris.

My daughter sometimes would hold my arm walking beside me carefully to the door. She would make sure to say hello to everyone and be sure not to forget to say: 'Mother, I will get your newspaper before picking you up for home.' Sometimes, she even kissed me on my cheek. That also was one reason I liked to come here; in those moments, I felt loved and showed I was loved. People said often that Aunty Doris deserved to have such a filial daughter.

Her friend Carol would wait in the car, as always. Carol was Mrs Chan's kitchen staff. She lived in staff accommodation. One day Astrid asked me, 'Mother, can we let Carol live in our spare room? She is the only woman living with three men.'

It was a good idea; my daughter could have a companion. I also thought it was true that being an only girl around those men at night wasn't safe. Then, Carol moved in and stayed in our small bedroom. Soon she moved into Astrid's bedroom, the biggest bedroom with large windows facing Meadows Park.

Astrid started to wear work slacks with sweaters and flat shoes; no more heeled shoes, no more makeup, and she put on a lot of weight. Her style became much more like Carol's. Then she decided to resign from her secretary job.

Carol started to call me 'Mum' and I would answer happily. I thought that I'd got another daughter.

When Carol was promoted to be a chef, Astrid became a head waitress; they were working for someone else's restaurant. My daughter was kicking the kitchen door in and out, yelling the table number and calling for sweet and sour chicken. They made a strong team and moved around from this restaurant to others in the towns. I could barely conceal my enormous disappointment. What she had learned from those nine years of expensive private boarding school and three years of secretary courses, had become such a waste.

'Hi Aunty Doris,' Jane rushed out from the office and opened her arms widely. Her smile could light up my grey mood. I was lucky to become a friend of Jane; she said to me that I was like her mother who lived in China she only went to see once a year. Jane hugged me warmly and asked me as usual: 'How are you, Doris?'

'The same. You know.' I sat down on the seat by the window in the large dining room and faced the door. People would say that was Aunty Doris's seat.

'Doris, you can't live like that. I am worried about you. If you fall, you could have broken bones or something,' said Jane, sitting next to me, lowering her voice. I regretted calling her when I had no one to call. I shouldn't have dragged her into my life.

'It won't be that easy to fall,' I was trying to be relaxed.

'Doris, I don't understand—why don't you just ask them to leave your house? It is your home,' she asked.

'Can you take me to my solicitor after lunch another day?' I said, changing the subject.

'Is it that will again?' Jane looked at me with sadness. She took a long breath then said, 'Doris, all those things are yours, you can do what you want to. Yes. Of course, I will take you there.'

Jane was a lawyer in China. She got her student visa in the Beijing British Embassy in 1989 when Tiananmen Square was occupied by students.

'The young officer in the embassy just asked me a few simple questions during the interview, then he told me to wait for half an hour and he would get my visa ready. I don't even know what he was talking about,' Jane told us. 'Then he showed me his watch, his finger pointed at the time—my God, my English was so bad, poor me,' she laughed. She joked that she wished she could meet this young officer again and speak to him in fluent English one day

There were rumours about how Jane got her permanent resident visa. Mrs Lee told me: 'She was married to a British man who worked as a cook in the same restaurant. A fake marriage, paid for with three thousand pounds.' I never asked Jane anything about those rumours. People who have left home always have their own reasons. Whether it is sweet or it is bitter. Only they know whether it is worth doing everything in their power. Now she worked hard as a part-time worker for Cathay Court, the residential accommodation for senior citizens including the Chinese.

She had her own story to tell, and I was a good listener.

Jane studied law at university. In the 1980s, when China resumed the lawyer qualification exam, she was one of those people who sat in the first exam room. 'I came first in my law firm,' she said with pride, 'I always thought the law was supreme, but, as what the professor said: books are far from reality.'

Her father was a famous doctor in their city. He was born and grew up in Indonesia and was sent to Guangzhou to study medicine by his parents, who, like most overseas Chinese, had great hopes for New China at the beginning of the fifties. After graduation, Jane's father obeyed the state assignment, and went to a small city with his newly wedded wife, becoming the first doctor who had a university degree in the only hospital, 'The People's Hospital'. Jane's father became vice-president of the hospital later and was well-respected.

One day, Jane's father was called from the ward to the office by the party secretary. Two plainclothes police officers had been his patients but pretended not to know him. They asked him how many letters he had written to his overseas sisters and what else was in the contents apart from family matters. They were taking notes, and ordered him to press down a red fingerprint at the end of the pages.

'My father did write about some of the things he saw, such as the obstetrics department throwing an aborted baby into the toilet bins. Doris, I have seen it too, not just once, but many times—the babies' feet and hands would kick around,' Jane said while gesturing, the horror on her face still sharp.

'My father often groaned about it a lot. My mother kept warning him to be careful with what he said. Maybe he didn't have anyone else to talk to. Then, he wrote to his sisters who lived in America; he thought it was safe to talk to them.'

The police finally warned Jane's father not to talk about things that hurt the image of China to the world. Birth control was the Party's policy and the whole country must follow it.

Soon, there was a new family that moved into the building where Jane's family lived. The husband was an administrator at the hospital, the wife was a hospital receptionist, and they also had a young daughter. They took the apartment above Jane's and soon they became Jane's family's close friends.

Years passed. In the nineties, one day, Jane's father was suddenly taken away by the police from his office and sent to a detention centre in Guangzhou, the provincial capital, in a prisoner van. No one explained to them why.

Jane found out where her father was held after a lot of help from people who were his patients or his patients' friends. The last words of her father were: 'Leave this country, go anywhere, just not here.' Jane's father died that night in his cell. Jane's family was told he died of a heart attack. He was never charged with any crimes.

Nearly two years later, Jane came to Edinburgh to study English; then stayed and opened a restaurant with her husband she met in Edinburgh, who also came from China as a student.

Jane said that during a Chinese New Year when she went back to China to see her mother, their upstairs neighbour confessed to them that, during those years, he had been their family's spy. His job was to keep eyes and ears on each of them. Those letters between her father and his sisters were all opened and checked.

'Oh, Doris, I had brought him a bottle of scotch whisky every time I went back. What a good neighbour!' Jane laughed with tears, wiping and wiping. 'You know why he told us? Because he was dying of lung cancer, even though he wasn't a smoker.'

It was afternoon teatime after lunch, when everybody played mahjong in the dining room, happily shouting at each other. Jane and I were sitting in the glass house which was in the middle of the two-storey building. The sadness on Jane's face was beyond expression, but her face was with a smile. I realised that the laughing, sunshine Jane was carrying such a heavy heart.

'You know Doris, I almost didn't make my way here, I... nearly jumped from the sixth floor of my office. Because I was like a lot of people in Guangzhou who joined the street demonstrations supporting those students who went on hunger strikes in Tiananmen Square. I was just one of those people in Guangzhou at that time. Then suddenly things started to change without notice.'

Jane was impersonally criticised by some of her colleagues and she was forced to self-criticise and write a confession as well. The last day before she left the law firm's office, the head of the Communist Party came to her desk and said, 'Do you really think you can get away from us even if you are leaving for England?'

'I was going to be like that... *Whoosh*... Down,' she was smiling but had tears in her eyes. My heart almost stopped. It brought back sad memories of my brother Gok suffering from the political turmoil in China. I realised that the political madness had never changed, actually. What a party my brother was so desperate to join.

I hugged Jane again before I walked out of the glass doors. She waved her hand with the same smile as usual.

Astrid and Carol were waiting in the car outside as normal. A Hong Kong-published weekend newspaper and a free magazine lay on the back seat.

'Those mainland women are so competitive, they always want to better themselves,' Astrid said, looking at Jane from the back window.

'People are poor in mainland China, they won't give up any chances,' Carol added.

'The restaurant she runs with her husband is very good business, I heard that they are going to open another one in the town centre.'

'They shouldn't be greedy, to be honest. I won't work for them.' Carol took a look in the mirror. She said that to me, I knew. I wasn't surprised.

Carol never liked those Chinese who came from mainland China. To her, they were the same kind of people who confiscated her family's belongings in Shanghai in 1950. Those people were poor and greedy, determined and lazy, fussy and disputing; no matter who it was, whether the doctors or the young girl washing the dishes in the kitchen, they were all wrong. Because, Carol and her family could never forget what the Communist Party had done to them in Shanghai. Her parents had to pay a huge amount of gold for their eight children and two servants, and fled to Hong Kong on the last ship. When her mother's jewellers were sold out, the former precious young lady Carol along with her sisters and brothers, had to look for a job to earn money. Carol was a kitchen helper working in a tearoom. By chance, she got a UK work visa and became Mrs Chen's second chef despite not knowing how to cook. Now my daughter was poisoned by Carol and joined her in her hatred which had expanded to the country and the people who were from it. It made me sad and angry.

'The only good person in the mainland is my uncle Gok—others? No one else,' Astrid said many times to please Carol. My brother sent a lot of Wen Nan green tea because once Astrid mentioned that tea could help reduce weight. She couldn't hate him.

'Don't forget you eat rice, not bread,' I couldn't help but rage. 'You two are Chinese.'

'Then why did you marry my father and live in England not China? If you don't like *gweilo*, if you love China, you should go back there Mother, shouldn't you?' Astrid raised her voice when Carol gave me an unhappy look.

'Yes, that is right. Mum, I don't understand—and you keep saying that you wanted to be a spy for China when you were the wife of a Scottish man,' Carol added calmly. They were allies, always. I couldn't help but say once: 'You used to love China, Astrid. You liked Chairman Mao—you even bought those little red books, they are still in your storeroom.'

'Where?' Astrid started to get mad again. When we arrived home she rushed upstairs, stormed into the storeroom, and overturned everything to prove I was wrong. She didn't want to find the red books, she just wanted to be angry at me. She was angry at anything which she felt might cause Carol unhappiness.

It had been like this for years. In the end, it was always Carol cleaning Astrid's mess, and Astrid's mother shut up. Trying to reason with them only enraged her even more. I learned to be mute and deaf whenever I needed to get my peace. So, I sat in the kitchen and let them be.

That was the last time I went to the senior lunch club, a place I could breathe and had a bit of laughter in my later life.

Taking me to my solicitor after lunch one day, as I arranged with Jane, didn't happen—because I didn't make it.

15. The Secret Revealed

15.1. The Mother

Seventy billion DNA connects mother and daughter. My daughter Astrid and I don't share this number. How many we do share, I don't know. How sad. I taught her my way through life to be the person I wanted her to be. But DNA is much more powerful. She has never been like me. If she was like me at all, it was just because she could hide herself very well.

In the winter of 1950, Hong Kong was especially cold. Strong wind from the north felt like a knife. I had put a large burning charcoal basket by our bedside at night. 'We may have smoky black faces in the morning, and smell like roast ducks,' Andrew joked. Sometimes, he did have a funny side.

After four years of civil war in the mainland between Mao and Chiang Kai-shek, Hong Kong became a safe place for those who were wealthy in China. They left everything behind them, taking only valuable personal belongings and the deeds of property and land, hoping one day that they could get them back. They could be super rich, like owners of the Bank of Shanghai, or own only a few acres of rice fields. They were afraid of being executed by the Communist Party. For a few years in Hong Kong, you would hear those well-dressed people, who spoke Mandarin or Shanghai dialect, proudly move in and out of the finest hotels. Particularly those people who came from Shanghai. You may have seen a man in an expensive suit and shiny leather shoes shouting haughtily to his servant in Shanghainese—a language Hong Kong people wouldn't understand. Then before very long, you may have seen a woman wearing a mink coat in a pawnshop begging for more money for her heavy gold bracelet; or a suited man asking for a job in a sauce-making factory. The lustre on them was all gone within days in the pawnshop. They would become one of us, working hard to live their lives. Carol and her family were just like one of them.

That evening, it was February 1950, near Chinese New Year. The road was jolly, filled with people who had started to shop for New Year. All the shops hung lanterns, one bigger than another, and colourful lightbulb chains hung from the top of the buildings.

At the very busy dry seafood store, turn right. There, was a baby's delivery clinic run by nuns. A man sat on a chair in a small room. He wore a dark Chinese-style cotton-padded jacket, torn sleeves showing grey cotton; under a pair of wide-leg hemmed trousers, his bare feet stepped into a pair of worn-out black leather shoes. He kept looking down when the nuns came in and out.

A woman's painful groaning intermittently passed through a door. Then a baby cried, weak, like a cat meowing. The nun came in, and the man looked up.

'Your wife wants you to go home. A girl. She doesn't want her,' the nun said in fluent Chinese. 'We will send her to an orphan asylum if there are no adoptive parents.'

The man just sat there like wood: dull, callous and indifferent, then his face became red. He stood up and walked out the door.

'Your wife will go home in the morning; she lost quite a lot of blood,' the nun raised her voice behind him. The man didn't turn back and didn't say a word.

Rows and rows of boats were floating on water at Yau Ma Tea dock, vacillating and staggering in waves. The Tanka people lived on these boats, fishing for a living. They were the original residents of Hong Kong. The famous picture of Victoria Five Miles was used for Hong Kong flags, government seals, and police emblems, and was printed on the Hong Kong currency. Designed by Messrs. Thomson & Son of Wapping in

1868, it told the story of a woman who guided the English army into Hong Kong. She was a wife of the Tanka people. When the army officer asked her what this village was called, she told him: 'Hong Kong'. She didn't know that since then, people would call this place 'Hong Kong', using actually the pronunciation from her dialect—Hakka, the local dialect the Tanka speak.

In the light of an oil lamp, people could see the man jumping into a pulling boat shoreside. Then he got into one of those boats.

'What did your woman have? Boy or girl?' an old woman popped up and asked.

'A girl. Dead.' The man crossed over his three children, lay down and covered himself with a heavy quilt.

'Died? How? I thought the foreign midwives were good. What a waste! I told your woman to do it on our boat. She has already done it three times. Where is your woman now? How much is it for her to stay overnight in that foreign place?...' The old woman still wanted to continue asking.

'Mother, go back to sleep, please don't say anything again,' the man broke in.

Next early morning, the man went fishing at sea, possibly for days.

Twelve months before, in busy Wan Chai, filled with the British and American Navies, their ships were docking at Victoria Harbour. Those men who wore white and blue uniforms were hanging around the shops, bars and restaurants, and yes, some were hiding in the red-light places where girls spoke broken English.

There was a sailor who worked as a chef. Short, fat and strong. He liked painting. Mostly he painted portraits. He was sitting on the deck, facing the docks, pencil flying on paper. Every time he saw this woman walking to the ship, he smiled and called out, 'Hi Mrs Kim, you *lei ho len* (look beautiful) today.'

When she left, he said, 'Wow you have many clothes to wash today. Good business. Ha.'

She said, 'Not much today. I wish I could get more.'

'I can help you. Are you coming the day after?'

The day after, she saw a lot of dirty clothes beside his chair. One day he asked her to let him paint her. In that kitchen store room, they started their relationship. This relationship traded with bunches of dirty clothes around his feet. The woman got pregnant. He gave her some money and said, 'Could be your husband's.' Then the painter disappeared.

The woman was told that he had gone back to America. The baby girl arrived nearly at the end of the Year of the Tiger, 1950. Her mother was one of Pauline's closest friends. It was Pauline who found the place where the baby was delivered for the mother.

'If the baby is your husband's, take the baby home; if not, leave her there. Those nuns will solve it,' Pauline said to the mother.

15.2. A Baby Girl Came Home

Three days after this unwanted and shameful baby girl arrived into this world, I was standing in front of the large rusted metal gate of the baby's delivery clinic with Pauline.

In those three days, I did so many things.

Day one—I told my Andrew.

'Are you sure darling? Where does this girl come from? Who are her parents? Why she does need to be adopted? What am I going to tell people?' Andrew looked shocked.

'I can't have children, you know that, and I don't want people to know it—and this girl has the look that matches us. Andrew, this is a chance right here: right baby, right time—I don't want to let it go,' I said desperately. It seemed I was convincing Andrew, but also myself more too.

I was old enough for people to gossip about me having no children. I knew women were always the only ones blamed, and that women should be ashamed of being unable to give birth.

'Darling, you know you can do anything you want. I am always there for you. Yes, why don't we bring up her as our own.'

Day two—I must find a place to move, somewhere no one knows us.

Luckily, I found a house for rent far away from the city, at Diamond Hill. There were only three stone-made houses at the corner. It suited us perfectly.

Day three. In the morning, I went to the Sincere department store where I bought baby goods. I bought a silk cape, clothes in pink and white with petite flowers, and two large tins of Cow & Gate milk powder, with two bottles. In the afternoon, I cut mine and Andrew's old cotton underclothes to make nappies.

A very old nun came to open the gate after Pauline rapped on the metal. She had a wrinkled face like crinkled paper that had been smoothed out again.

'Oh, Miss Keung, this must be your sister, Mrs Devlin?' She spoke perfect Cantonese. 'Come with me.'

Through the light from the other taller buildings, I could see there was a skylight courtyard, and a few potted plants trembling in the cold. Around the yard, there were closed doors painted in a khaki colour, and peeling walls. A low and deep groaning was emanating heavily from the third door on the right. Then, the whole place was back to a stressful silence.

The nun opened the first door on the left-hand side gently. She turned on the light which hung from the ceiling. Under the faint light I saw four small beds, three were empty. A tiny thing was wrapped up in a towel, sleeping under a large quilt. The room was cold.

'Here she is,' the nun said, sighing heavily. 'She is quite weak; not much crying. Would you like to take a look?' she looked at me.

I was standing with my heart beating fast; at that moment I was faltering. I saw a tiny face with long eyelashes and no high nose bridge like a foreigner's. She breathed evenly and had a familiar smell, like my little sister's. To my surprise she had no hair, only a few pieces of dirt, stuck on her head. I thought of how I could wash them away.

'May, she looks cute. Babies grow up in days. Trust me,' Pauline whispered.

'I will take her home,' I nodded my head.

'Oh, how wonderful! You have a good heart. This girl is lucky,' the nun smiled. An English husband and a Chinese wife adopted a mixed-race baby at the right time—what else could make the nun happier but have this perfect match?

'Her mother didn't have any clothes for her. The blanket is ours. If you have your own, we would like to take it back,' the sister said. All she had was the worn-out towel wrapping her and one nappy made out of a wheat flour bag. There wasn't any paperwork needed.

The gate closed behind us in the dark, it was a dull kind of regular sound that came from rust.

We got on the bus and went home. Pauline carried the baby on her back. The red baby sling woven with peony flowers was far too big.

Pauline turned her back to me and said, 'Look at her, doesn't she look like your husband and a little bit like you?' I moved the silk blanket; her little face was right down against Pauline's back. I was worried she would not be able to get her breath. I took my gloves off and turned her head around to face me. She was so peacefully in a deep sleep. Her face looked pink. I took her hand out carefully, stroking.

'Oh, her nails are long,' I told Pauline.

'Don't clip them yet. Wait till she is one month old.'

'I wonder, what colour hair she will grow up with?' Andrew has chestnut colour hair, I very much hoped she had the same colour.

'All the foreigners have similar hair, May,' Pauline said. 'If my little pilot was not dead, he would be seventeen this year, you know.'

'Pauline, you know, this is a secret to keep for our lifetimes.' I looked into Pauline's eyes.

'May, are you crazy? Why would I tell? Who am I?' Pauline's big hand smacked my shoulder.

Yes, I trusted her. She swore to me the cruellest oath to make me trust her. She said if she revealed this secret, she would be killed by a thundering lightning strike. It was the strictest self-imposed spell in Chinese culture.

Andrew was waiting at the door. He was very nervous; I could see him stepping in and out of the cold.

'We will call her Astrid.' He stared at our baby with a fatherly smile that I had never seen and held her close to his chest stiffly. 'My mother was called Astrid.' It made me almost cry.

I gave two hundred dollars to Pauline. 'Give this money to the mother, it may help her a little. What is her family name?'

'Kim, Aunty Kim.'

That night I bathed her with warm water in a big wooden tub. I was so scared of breaking her arms, and legs—they were so small, like Andrew's thumbs.

All night, Andrew and I nearly had no sleep at all. We were worried something bad was going to happen to this tiny baby. We took turns to stare at her while she was sleeping. We were exhausted and excited.

When I looked at them both, I couldn't stop imagining the future we would have ahead of us together.

This girl is mine, her name is Astrid Devlin.

Her father is Andrew Devlin, from Scotland.

Her mother is May Hou, from Heng Tin village in Guangdong, China.

Her brown hair will be divided in the middle, tied with a pink ribbon on both sides.

She will wear a dress like those displayed at the windows of Lane Crawford.

She must go to a good school and learn to play the piano.

She will become a well-mannered young lady, working in an office like those secretary girls in pencil skirts and black high-heeled shoes.

Then she will meet a good man, marry him and have three children.

No one is going to know her secret, only her parents and her dearest Aunty Pauline. No one else, not even herself.

15.3. She Isn't Your Mother

Years and days can give you what you want but also take something from you, slowly, without a sound.

I was sitting in the kitchen and staring at my small television. It was getting dark even at only nearly four in the afternoon. I wondered if my daughter would be home for dinner after a heated row between mother and daughter over silly things.

Pauline called me last night and said, 'Astrid is in my house, and Carol too. I don't understand why you always want her to find another job. What is wrong with waitressing? They will be home tomorrow.'

Eventually, I heard the key turning in the door lock. Astrid came into the kitchen while Carol walked up the stairs. I could see her eyes were so red and swollen.

She stood by the kitchen door and asked, 'Tell me the truth—am I your birth daughter? Or am I your adopted daughter?' She seemed calm, surprisingly.

No words could come out of my mouth. I was frozen on the chair. Only laughter came from the television, at the wrong time.

An inconsolable sobbing from Astrid's room; and Carol's gentle voice.

I walked to Pauline's home.

'You vowed,' I shouted at Pauline, trying so hard to hold back my tears, clasping my shaking hands, but they still couldn't help but roll down. Pauline turned her head to look out of the window and said, 'You have done things that hurt me, you know.'

'What things? Anything, you tell me?' My brain couldn't think of anything. She couldn't answer.

'Only one thing's for sure: you just can't bear that—my life seems better than yours,' I said.

'Yes, of course. You have your Astrid with you here, your daughter. Everyone knew my daughter was adopted. Now she has abandoned me for America with her husband and sons. Didn't even ask me to live with them. Do you know how lonely I am? How helpless I am?' Pauline started to cry dolefully.

'You intentionally let her sleep with the American tenant when she was only seventeen. Do you remember you said to me that was your idea?' I fought back for once. 'You were planning to keep him in Edinburgh to help you to run a restaurant.'

'Yes! Look now, they are all gone,' Pauline wiped her tears with her shirt hem. She whimpered in grievance, 'I have given all my properties under her name, hoping she will be grateful and come back to Edinburgh. You know, May, I haven't seen them for over a year. My grandchildren don't even want to talk to me. They don't speak Chinese anymore. They are American.'

I sat heavily on her torn sofa and couldn't find any words. Sadness, for her, for myself, was swelling in my heart.

'You tell me—what am I going to do? You tell me, tell me?' I muttered to myself more than to Pauline. I heard my voice cracking and quivering hoarsely.

'I have kept your secret for long enough. I think you should be grateful,' she said sternly, 'Astrid should know the truth. She is nearly forty. Not a child anymore.'

'The truth? The truth that was she was a shameful child—that she was an abandoned child? You know she can't face the facts. It will kill her,' I raised my voice angrily. 'And you know clearly that she has nowhere to go, you know we don't know where her birth mother is now. If there is a reason why she must know, let me tell her.'

'We said a lot of things when we were young, May,' she said with a little deprecating shrug.

Quiet, both of us went quiet.

We were staring at the television. A popular Hong Kong show, *A Family Love Bond,* was playing on Pauline's small television on videotape. I rented it for her.

'Do you have any contact with your friend who knew Aunty Kim, Astrid's birth mother?' I broke the silence.

'I don't. Since I moved to England we gradually lost contact, one by one. You know I can't write. The telephone costs a lot.' Pauline was deflated. 'What is the big deal? At least I didn't tell anyone that Astrid is… A lesbian,' she added.

'Who says that she is?' It was another shock to me.

'Everyone knows about it. You just didn't want to know,' she said with a self-satisfied smile.

'You and I have shared a char siu bao, we have shared a bed—are we lesbians?' I stood up. 'They keep their bedroom door open, always… You are jealous of me, you always have been.'

The wind dragged me into the darkness as I walked out of Pauline's house. On the way home in the dark, I felt regret flood deeply over my mind. For everything I did and for everything I didn't do.

Since that day, I hardly spoke to Pauline anymore. My adopted daughter Astrid moved out with Carol to the apartment they bought together. Before she moved into their new home, she and Carol stayed in Pauline's house. Her aunt Pauline's nine-bedroom house truly had plenty of space. Astrid and Carol sometimes came home to collect their things but hardly spoke to me. It seemed there was no more to talk about. Everything started to change in subtle ways, at least I felt that way.

Pauline's daughter never came back to live in Edinburgh. Only once a year would she return to visit her mother.

Pauline's tenants all moved out because she vacuumed at midnight, and advised the student tenants that there was no need to take showers every day, because England was not as hot as Hong Kong. Most of the time she was cleaning, from the basement to the top floor, and then from the top floor to the basement.

16. I Have Gone Home at Last

16.1. Only Days I Had Left

Summer nearly ended.

Autumnal winds and rains had come early.

Mournful yellow leaves were falling and floating.

Some of them touched down on the roof of my house.

Years after years, water started to drop from the large glass rooftop. My beautiful stone staircase always had a few buckets on it from when it was raining over the past ten years. First one, then two, then more. 'Get another bucket from under the sink!' Carol shouted when it was heavy rain.

I was sitting on my chair in the kitchen, drinking tea with a piece of toast and watching my old television. Carol called it 'your television'; she called the large one in the living room 'our television'. They seemed to forget that both televisions were mine; even the house they had lived in for many years since they moved back, was mine too. Their apartment was rented out for a good rental income in their pockets.

I heard Astrid rush into the kitchen. She was still wearing her pyjamas. She pulled out a metal bucket from under the sink and then rushed out.

'The stairs are all wet and easy to slip down—it's dangerous for her,' Astrid said with a bit of concern.

'She isn't blind, she will see it,' Carol replied.

She must have had the same smile on her face, which was always very convincing. Everyone in the house knew that her smiles weren't real.

'Your mother is only a little bit deaf,' Carol added.

They said it was impossible to find a good roofer to repair such damaged old glass. I knew what they were thinking. They thought that this house was going to be put on the market for sale. Just the right time hadn't come yet, but it would soon.

They cooked their meals and ate in the living room. They watched television while they were eating and talking. I stayed in my place: the kitchen.

This started about four months ago. One evening, Pauline's daughter Debra and her two sons came to visit while they were back from America to see Pauline. I gave three red paper envelopes to them as usual. This time inside each one was a fifty-pound note.

'Lucky money, here you are. Safe journey back home. You are all good kids,' I said.

'Oh yes—keep it, keep it, make my mother happy, you know her, Debra,' Astrid said to them after Debra's sons smiled sweetly and said there was no need because they were too old to receive lucky money from me anymore like they had used to. Astrid insisted, and put them into their pockets one by one.

When the door closed behind Debra, Astrid started to tidy up in the kitchen and her anger had started too. 'You seem to have too much money?' She was putting the teacups into the sink loudly. 'You tell me, am I your daughter or Debra?' Astrid stood with her back to the sink and faced me.

Her face looked pale. Her eyes became red. She would cry any second. She may follow through by smashing the teacups. I was so used to seeing her like this, losing her mind over just little things. I must leave the kitchen, go to my room and lock my door, I thought.

'Where are you going, Mother? Listen to me!' Astrid was ranting from the kitchen and grabbed me from behind on the staircase. I was forced to take two steps back; I was going to fall if I slipped off the cast-iron rail.

'Are you mad?' Carol pushed Astrid into the living room. 'You won't get a penny from her if you carry on treating her like this.'

The door closed behind them. Following it Astrid cried hysterically.

I sat down on my bed and tried to not cry. My hands were shaking. I was thinking about whether I should press the elderly alarm button this time, and wait for the police to come or whoever to come—but then what would happen to them? If those sleeping pills in my bedside drawer I had saved up were working still, maybe it was time to swallow them all tonight. Then I started to worry about Astrid; she told me often she would die before me because her sleeping pills hadn't expired.

That night I took extra sleeping pills to force myself to get into a deep sleep.

In the early morning. I was awakened by noise.

'Astrid has had a stroke.' Carol looked panicked.

My daughter was on a stretcher carried by two male paramedics. Her eyes behind her glasses were opened widely and looked at me. I knew she wanted to say something to me, but no words came out of her mouth, her face was full of fear. That fear, I had seen before when she was seven years old in Hong Kong. She was nearly attacked by a snake in a field. It was me who pulled her behind my back and who threw a rock at that big snake. That night Astrid had a fever, she was ill for a few days.

Looking at her terrified face on the stretcher, my heart sank. I held her hand and stroked her face and told her, 'Don't be scared, I am here, darling.' She nodded her head.

'Quick, quick.' Carol jumped into the ambulance and gave me that look: your fault.

A week later, Astrid came home. I became the one blamed.

Since the secret came out that Astrid was my adopted daughter, I was the most selfish adoptive mother, who was scared of being abandoned in her old age. Because I had refused to tell Astrid where her birth mother was, what her mother's name was, and of those siblings she may have had.

No one mentioned anything else about what was going on behind my door. Nor did I. The only person I told was Jane, because she was unlike my other friends. She didn't play mahjong nor did she gossip.

16.2. The Way to Meet My Andrew

September 3rd. It was dull and slightly drizzly when my hearse left the Oakvale funeral home, which had previously been my daughter's old school. She had spent nine years there. Andrew and I had only been a few times for parent evenings.

Andrew did his best to walk through the rocky pathway in the front garden. I was so afraid that he was going to fall; that would have been embarrassing for our daughter. All the parents were very polite and kind, and followed us walking as slowly as Andrew.

The garden today looked the same as when I used to see Astrid playing with her school friends. When I took the number twelve bus intentionally, which passed by the school, I would sit on the upper deck by the window, wishing that I could see her playing in the garden. Now, this girl's school had become an expensive funeral service, my funeral held in their largest room. It was my daughter's choice. A roomful of people came to say goodbye for the last time.

Everything seemed the same here, apart from those trees. They had all grown higher and bigger, covering up the sky. Leaves had fallen to the sodden grass. Astrid's large *MUM* wreath was on top of my brown solid wood coffin. The wreath was made from beautiful white chrysanthemums. Astrid ordered them from the flower shop, opposite Steve's Fish & Chips shop.

Only a few days before while I stood outside the fish & chip shop for the last time, eating deep-fried crispy cod in the wind, I couldn't forget that fish & chips was the first meal I had in Edinburgh that night we arrived to this city from London back in 1946. It had become one of my favourite English meals.

Across the road, I saw a lady very busy making these *MUM* wreathes. 'She must have seen many sad people through the years,' I thought. Now, it was my time.

When I was lying on the hospital bed, Astrid kissed my forehead like she used to do.

'Shh, shh… Peaceful now, Mother, no more hurt, no more,' she whispered in my ear. Tears rolling down her face. She stroked my right hand where there was a big blue patch on the back. The doctors tried hard to save me from a leaking heart. They told Astrid the blood pumped out from my heart had gone everywhere in my body.

That morning, Carol took a look at me in the kitchen and went out. She said to Astrid, 'She doesn't look good, Astrid, your mother.'

Astrid was just getting ready to attend her medical appointment for a follow-up check-up after her stroke. I was trying to get up to make one piece of toast, but I couldn't. Astrid asked, 'Where do you feel isn't right?'

'Only my right leg is painful,' I said.

'It must be caused by you walking up to Steve's Fish & Chips shop in the last couple of days.' Carol seemed relieved. 'We did tell you that you shouldn't eat those fatty things.' She paused for a bit, then carried on. 'You know, our meals are not suitable for you. Why you don't cook your own?'

'We will keep you some chicken tonight,' Astrid said to Carol, who was standing by the door with car keys in her hand.

I heard them close the door. Then the door opened again. 'I'll give my appointment to you, Mother.' Astrid came into the kitchen.

I was only preparing to leave home to see my GP, I never thought I wouldn't return home again. There was no need for Astrid to keep a piece of chicken for her mother.

The hearse carried on, driving slowly along those streets. Those shops, every tree and bush at each corner, they were witnesses; they saw a little woman, always in a hurry to scramble for a living, watching her from a young woman become old—*goodbye*, I said.

The hearse stopped outside my home. The pink door was in silence. Joy and sadness happened behind this door for forty-six years. It seemed Andrew was sitting by the window smiling, just like that day in St. Mary's Church in Hong Kong—*goodbye*, I said.

The Meadows Park's September was being squeezed slowly out of its teeming life. Winter came much earlier. Day after day, season after season, the sunshine, the rain, the snow, this all, I have seen it and felt it—*goodbye*, I said.

My camphor trunk must still be sitting in the corner of the living room. It has done its job—*goodbye*. I knew Astrid would certainly find these things inside: my wedding dress with a pair of long silk gloves, which I was wearing as was my wish; a large brown envelope, which was the deed of the grave I bought for the three of us. She needed it to bury me. My favourite *cheongsams*. Inside my most beloved black and gold long *cheongsam* coat, which was made of the best silk, she would find my fragmented marriage certificate wrapped inside. She also would find her father's favourite brown lamb shearling jacket, which I altered down to my size after Andrew died, and had worn for years. I was glad my dear friend Mrs Chan asked Astrid to put it on me because I might feel cold inside the coffin. What a good idea. And also Astrid would see her christening dress and a pair of her tiny socks wrapped inside a pink blanket among her wool hat I knitted, similar to my sister's. They all had become yellowed like my wedding dress, but no damage.

I knew she would be disappointed too because she wouldn't see any scraps of writing about her when I took her home sixty-one years ago. There was not a single thing from her biological mother. I was telling her the truth: there was nothing.

We both forgot how many times she said, 'I don't believe you!' Once Astrid screamed, 'You must swear an oath on this Bible.' She put down the Bible on the table vigorously and insisted that I must press my hand on it to swear that 'I do not know who Astrid's birth mother is and where she is.' I didn't do it. Because, to me, I didn't lie, so I did not need to attest to the Bible.

Sadly, Astrid chose not to believe me and gave herself a reason to release her anger and pain. All my explanations were deliberately and increasingly wrangled over by her excuses till I began to keep my silence.

Meanwhile, there was no will. Astrid was expecting it would be found inside the camphor trunk.

The sunshine suddenly poured in through the drizzle when the hearse finally arrived at my grave where Andrew was waiting. I was wearing my wedding dress and my long gloves, just like that day in Hong Kong.

My coffin was rolled down to my grave by my nephew—Gok's son, who settled in England as his father wished. He got married and had children in this country that I was trying to leave and which had been regarded as my home, eventually.

Hold me tight Owen. My dear brother-in-law Owen was at the front of my coffin.

Owen retired from a high-ranking officer position in the Inland Revenue. He then became a chair of the Edinburgh Ambulance Service. Just not long ago, we had dinner together in a buffet restaurant. Owen joked, 'I still have that cowboy shotgun belt. It's still as new as when you bought it for me.' It was a gift I bought for his tenth birthday. He was thrilled when he opened the wrapping, and immediately put it around the waist with his head held high. 'You never see me as grown up, Doris, do you?' Owen laughed, 'I am going to let my grandson inherit your cowboy gun.' What a well-worthy gift.

To me, Owen was always nine years old. I still remember the nine-year-old who asked me, 'Doris, can you teach me kung fu? I read a book that said Chinese people can fly over the eaves and walk around the walls; and they shout and stretch their arms, sweep their legs—lightning speed in the sky, then seven bad guys will fall.'

'Do I look like a kung fu person?' I couldn't help but laugh when I saw his seriousness. 'But, I can do some kicking and do somersaults. I trained in the theatre for two years.' Owen couldn't find anyone to teach him kung fu, instead he learned judo until he got a black belt. I knew that was because he felt he was a boy and wanted to protect his sisters and mother from his father. Then he joined the Royal Air Force, like his big old brother Andrew, and became a soldier.

Owen wrote to his brother, who was in Hong Kong, and told him that the night before he left home for the RAF, their father suddenly said sorry, and hoped that his sons would forgive what he had done; he was very proud of him and Andrew. Andrew was choked up in the throat when he read that.

Sarah, Jennie, Mary and Ann, my sisters-in-law, didn't come to my funeral. I wanted them to know that whenever they came back to Edinburgh from the United States to visit relatives, they would stay at my home first. They said that when their parents were not there anymore, then the home of their elder brother and elder sister-in-law was like their parents' home. It was so like the traditional ancient motto of the Chinese: when the parents are absent, the eldest becomes the father and his wife becomes the mother. It made me feel warm and loved by the Devlins.

Hold me tight Joe. My dear friend held the rope on the back of my coffin.

Joe was a true English gentleman; he was my house carpenter and electrician—overall, he was the handyman of my house. Precisely, he was more like Andrew's companion. I always remember that day he saved Andrew and our house.

That morning Joe came to fix our dripping water tap; I cooked mutton and vegetable soup for Andrew and him to have tea together. I forgot to turn off the fire before rushing to work. The big soup pot dried up and thick smoke was rolling. When Joe opened the front door, thick smoke billowed into the hallway—he had to crawl forward to the kitchen to turn off the gas cooker just before a fire started. Andrew was sleeping in the living room. That lunch, Joe and Andrew had a drink to celebrate the escape. I was glad that we let Joe have a set of my house keys. I regretted not telling Joe that it was such a warm comfort whenever I came home from work, to hear Joe and Andrew chatting and laughing. And as well, those phone calls from Joe brought a light to my grey days after Andrew passed away.

'Can we go out for coffee more often, Doris?' sometimes Joe would ask me. 'If you'd like,' he added. We didn't go out often, of course. Because my Astrid didn't like it. 'Mother, Joe seems to like to date you. Neighbours may gossip,' she said.

I didn't know how he knew that there was a funeral for me, because he had stopped coming for a few years. Joe came by, bravely knocked on the pink door, and told Astrid he must be one of the people to carry my coffin.

On the other side of the rope from Joe was Mr Lau.

He did his utmost to keep himself balanced rolling the rope as he was a short man. Mr Lau was educated and spoke fluent English. Spared no effort with his time and money on the Chinese community. He won the respect of the Chinese in Edinburgh and he also was a successful businessman. It was worth keeping a secret for many years.

It was unexpectedly in the department store. I saw him standing by the counter for school uniforms. Beside him was a little girl, about five years old. She was talking to him.

'Dad,' she called when Mr Lau carried some private girls ' school uniform while walking towards the cashier. I stopped at once and turned around. Because, Mr Lau didn't have a daughter—he had three sons with his Chinese wife. This girl had brown hair. She was of mixed parentage.

He must have given some excuse to get away from his restaurant on a busy Saturday and must have done that many times. The only thing I was worried about was when the day of exposure came, how many people would get hurt. Then I felt comforted that Mr Lau gave his secretly brought-up daughter the same education as her three half-brothers. Since that day I couldn't help but think about what that little girl is doing now. I wished she would be a doctor. To me, her father was a good man.

Where was Pauline? She said that she was older than me, and by tradition, it would bring her bad luck to bid farewell to her lifelong friend.

Dear Jane—it must be because I told you my secret, that you told me yours. You wanted me to know life was worth carrying on its purpose. I was glad we did that, even though we were not of the same generation and we had different life journeys too.

To my brothers—we will see each other again and be together again with our father and mother.

Don't cry. You all.

16.3. A Dream to My Daughter

The second time Lorna knelt before me, it was in Edinburgh in February, a cold morning. She came straight from Edinburgh airport to my grave and pleaded forgiveness for not coming to my funeral because her third husband was so ill. Wearing her brown mink coat, knees on the wet grass, she clasped her hands at her chest and said, 'Godmother, if there is a second life, I would be your goddaughter again.'

Buddha always said that only glancing back five hundred years in pre-existence could lead to such an encounter in this life. Only in my heart was I filled with a thousand regrets, hoping we could return to each other in the days and years of the afterlife. I also wanted to say this to my adopted daughter Astrid.

This year had to be the worst year for both of us, truly. On that day and many other days, you told me, 'I leave all that's mine to you in my will, Mother.' But I wondered what you had and what I wanted from you.

'Oh, Mother, Joe told me today that if this house is changed to be under my name earlier, I can avoid inheritance tax,' you said. I kept silent.

Then you shouted, 'Aunty Pauline has changed her property to be under Debra's name. I don't understand why you haven't yet?'

You started to get angry again, like every other time this came up.

'Debra is married and has two children,' I broke my silence.

'Yes, Mother, I don't have a husband like hers, I only have Carol, who you hate. I am sorry that I am the daughter you had adopted unluckily—not like Pauline's. I am also your daughter who didn't become what you were hoping for.' You began to lose your temper.

'Yes, I am wearing a sweater and jeans, flat shoes—let's see if I still have those dresses or pencil skirts you like.' You were running upstairs and downstairs looking for them, but there were no more because you had torn them all, then you were looking for something else you could tear. Those photos of you and me became your target. It wasn't enough, so then you dashed in and out of the kitchen where I was sitting, banging on the old table and kicking the old chairs. You continued to shout. Your face looked even more pale, and your eyes, like a cornered beast, were red; your short brown hair was messily greasy and sticky.

'You took me home, in fact—you bought me for two hundred Hong Kong dollars. It wasn't me who asked you to take me home.' You carried on releasing your indignation.

'Don't forget you have a responsibility to raise me and support me until the day I die. How dare you think you could sell this house and pay for your expensive nursing home? Do you really think I didn't know that you have been to the nursing home where the twin sisters on the lower ground floor are staying? Are you going to spend all the money on it? Why are you doing this to me?' You were bawling and exhausted.

'You always said how much money you spent on me for that private school. Did you know I was bullied frequently because I was a mixed-race girl? I was pressed down to the toilet and made to drink the dirty water. Those wealthy girls never liked me because we weren't wealthy.' You howled like a wounded animal. 'I didn't ask for those luxuries. Only you did.'

Finally, you ran out to the hall and ran into the living room, then to upstairs. 'I am leaving this time for real. We must leave her, Carol.' You packed your things and ran down.

'Where can we go, you idiot? Our apartment is still occupied,' Carol started to bellow at her.

Yes, where could you two go? Clever Carol was your brain, as always. You sat in the hallway with your large suitcase and cried hopelessly. Besides your cries, the only sound was the television. I walked out of the kitchen and stood in front of you. I felt sorry and sad.

'I was just thinking about it, just been thinking a little of selling this house for my care home. That's it.' I was comforting a sixty-one-year-old like a ten-year-old child.

I told you, 'I have left my rental income from the China Garden to you. That money can support you for the rest of your life and your Carol's. In the past for more than many years, that income has kept the house running for everyone. You know that, both of you.'

Your cries became sobs. I took a long sigh from my chest and said to you, 'I wish I had asked more about your mother. I wish at least I had kept that tiny nappy.' I walked upstairs in tears.

I looked through my bedroom window. Outside, the fading skylight was drained away by the ticking sounds of the clock on my bedside table, which you bought for me in Hong Kong. Forty years on, it still was working very well, unlike me.

The red and orange dahlias were blooming in the back garden. They were just like those in my far away hometown village. A newly moved-in young couple had bought the lower ground floor from the old twin sisters who sold their home to pay for a six-hundred-pound-a-week nursing home that Astrid was angry I might sell my house to pay for.

Last year, the young couple had worked hard to rebuild the abandoned backyard. They were expecting their first child. I guessed the kind and cheerful twins must have been very happy to see that.

Life comes and goes, certainly. And life's destiny ordains they are who they are, where they must be, who they will meet, and when the end would be. It is so true.

I didn't tell Astrid that I had been back to the place where she was born when I visited Hong Kong. There was nothing left I could recognise. I even wanted to seek out her family in the newspapers. I was hoping to find her mother to save Astrid from the pain and mine.

I would say to this woman: 'Your daughter, you left her in that room with a tiny nappy. Do you still remember her dirty little face? Have you been thinking of her at night? Did I raise her well?'

I would also say to her: 'Take her back. She has been looking for you for twenty-five years.'

I would also say to her: 'Tell your daughter what the old Chinese say: "Give birth without upbringing, a broken finger can return the debt you owe; upbringing without giving birth, it will take lifetimes to return the immense debts you owe.'

Those thoughts have been on my mind over and over.

My will has been changed many times. But one wish has never been changed: that the house must be sold to someone who would truly love it. So many people I loved, and so many people I owed a debt to in my lifetime. Like that hospital, which treated Andrew so well. The money from the sale of this house will show mine and Andrew's immense gratitude to them. Don't take Carol's advice to challenge my will, because you won't get what you and Carol were waiting for. I won't be sorry.

One night, I will appear to you in a dream, no matter whether you like it or not.

I was walking in the wind, wrapped around in a large black wool shawl. You were wearing your favourite dress which had cherry flowers all over. I made it in my bedroom in our home in that little stone house at Diamond Hill in Hong Kong.

I climbed on a low rock wall, looking over. There was a large meadowland. The rain was dropping from the sky as if thousands of water beads were sprinkling on the grass under the setting sun. That was the place where I played with my brothers and my cousins, like a boy. Chasing each other, rolling over, betting for candies. We always forgot to go home, until our names were called out by our mothers. I jumped on the wet grass, trying trickily to hop on the solid parts with my sandals.

'Mother, you must be careful!' I heard you shout behind me. You were standing on that low wall where I was standing. I turned around and shouted back, 'I am fine, do not worry about me!'

On the other side of the meadowland, over another low rock wall, there was a tall and slim tree, dense lemon-green leaves seemed to be singing in the sunset glow and breeze. I disappeared right there in front of you. Your face was covered up with tears and you were also smiling with relief.

Love is hope. Love is forgiveness. I want you and me to have it.

Postscript

My brother Gok died peacefully on a morning, about 5 a.m. in China. It was October 26th 2018, the day of my hundredth birthday. Before Gok fell into a coma in the hospital, he refused to sleep in his room in his bed. He insisted that his bed had a large hole in the middle, and he was going to fall, and the walls in his room were falling too. His ashes were carried back to the UK by his son. On a wintry sunny day, Gok's ashes were scattered into the River Mersey in Liverpool, the city where his sons and grandsons had settled. His daughter-in-law threw my comb into the water and shouted, 'Papa, your sister is here with you.' The ferryboat honked kindly. The water churned behind the ferry; waves broke white into flowers, gleaming in the dazzling sunlight, following at great speed along the Mersey River to merge with the sea. It was just as he wished, as per Gok's will: 'My ashes must go into the sea, any sea.'

Kai one day, packed everything and left Hong Kong for mainland China to the city Gok lived. He described his day to me over the phone. He said with a rare delightful voice, he was the one who put on the rice cooker every day. Gok was the one who went to the street market to buy fresh fish and vegetables every morning and cooked three meals a day. 'Gok cooked stuffed fish, just like our mother did,' he said. He drank almost his whole life like our father, which caused him to die of a brain haemorrhage. He didn't die alone. Gok was at his side. His ashes were buried beside our father on the mountain behind Heng Tin Village.

Owen, my brother-in-law very sadly had Alzheimer's disease in his later life. Died aged seventy-seven; he lived thirty years longer than his brother Andrew.